W9-DBZ-338

Phyllis W. Shofrow Ed. D.
1983

Report writing P. 100

A RORSCHACH INTRODUCTION
Content and Perceptual Approaches

A RORSCHACH INTRODUCTION
Content and Perceptual Approaches

EDWARD ARONOW, Ph.D.
Associate Professor of Psychology
Montclair State College and
Psychologist in Private Practice
Upper Montclair, New Jersey

MARVIN REZNIKOFF, Ph.D.
Professor and Chairman
Department of Psychology
Fordham University
Bronx, New York, and
Clinical Consultant for the State of Connecticut
Franklin S. Dubois Day Treatment Center
Stamford, Connecticut

GRUNE & STRATTON
A Subsidiary of Harcourt Brace Jovanovich, Publishers
New York   London
Paris   San Diego   San Francisco   São Paulo
Sydney   Tokyo   Toronto

Library of Congress Cataloging in Publication Data

Aronow, Edward.
   A Rorschach introduction.

   Bibliography: p. 124
   Includes index.
   1. Rorschach test.   I. Reznikoff, Marvin.   II. Title.
BF698.8.R5 A763   1983   155.2′842   82-21038
ISBN 0-8089-1516-9

Grune & Stratton, Inc.
111 Fifth Avenue
New York, New York 10003

**Distributed in the United Kingdom by
Academic Press Inc. (London) Ltd.**
24/28 Oval Road, London NW 1

Library of Congress Catalog Number 82-21038
International Standard Book Number 0-8089-1516-9
Printed in the United States of America

To Audrey, David, and Rebecca.
To Linda and all my children.

Contents

Acknowledgment

Reproduction of the Rorschach blots in the location sheets is by permission of Verlag Hans Huber Publishers, Bern, Switzerland.

Reproduction of the Klopfer location areas is by permission of Dr. Walter Klopfer and Harcourt Brace Jovanovich, Publishers.

Reproduction of the Beck list of populars is by permission of Grune & Stratton, Inc.

Introduction

As initially presented by Hermann Rorschach, the Rorschach test was conceived largely as a perceptual instrument, with the personality of the test subject revealed through scoring categories such as location, determinants, and form-level. Later, Rorschach clinicians such as Beck, Klopfer, and Piotrowski, continued this perceptual emphasis with content considerations typically given short shrift. In recent years, however, content interpretation began to receive more attention as it became evident that the validity literature was much more promising for content than for perceptual categories (e.g., Aronow & Reznikoff, 1976; Eron, 1965) and that clinicians relied quite heavily on content in interpreting test records (Potkay, 1971; Powers & Hamlin, 1957; Symonds, 1955). The purpose of this book is to provide a more balanced presentation of these two approaches to Rorschach work than is available in other contemporary introductory Rorschach texts that have without exception been based largely on an analysis of the perceptual components of the test.

Thus, the present text will attempt to do two things. First, the major perceptual scoring categories will be summarized to provide the proper ground for the student in the traditional Rorschach procedure. Chapter 1 discusses traditional administration techniques and what is known about the blot stimulus characteristics. Chapter 2 defines the response and the scoring of locations. The heart of traditional perceptual interpretation, the determinants category, is presented in Chapter 3, while form-level, the scoring of populars, and the simple content categories are discussed in Chapter 4. Tabulation and traditional perceptual interpretation are presented in Chapter 5. Chapter 6 concludes the perceptual section of this text with a brief summary of normative data pertinent to the scoring categories.

In the discussion of the traditional perceptual categories, we have chosen to follow primarily, but not exclusively, the Klopfer approach, bringing in contributions by other workers when indicated, such as the list of populars developed by Beck. We have also elected to simplify perceptual scoring and tabulation in an effort to make the presentation more understandable to the student and to eliminate the many convoluted aspects of scoring and tabulation that contribute to the psychometric deficiencies of the Rorschach technique.

In the second half of this book, the content approach to Rorschach interpretation is presented. Chapter 7 first discusses the theoretical underpinnings of content interpretation, in general, and idiographic content interpretation, in particular. Chapter 8 continues the discussion of idiographic content interpretation with an exposition on the weaknesses and problems of this approach along with 16 suggested guidelines designed to make idiographic content interpretation more productive and to reduce the occurrence of "wild analysis." Chapter 9 enlarges the presentation on idiographic interpretation by a discussion and elucidation of the important area of content sequence analysis. Finally, Chapter 10 discusses content-oriented techniques of test administration (in particular, the Content Rorschach Technique that we have developed). Chapter 11 presents report writing, and Chapter 12 contains two complete test protocols—one obtained by the traditional administration technique and one obtained by the Content Rorschach Technique.

As noted, the perceptual chapters of this book are presented prior to the idiographic content chapters in order to acquaint the student initially with the traditional technique. This order does not imply that we regard the perceptual categories of primary importance in interpretation. Rather, it is our view that the Rorschach should not be regarded basically as a test, but as a specialized type of clinical interview procedure, as suggested by Anastasi (1976). The major emphasis in arriving at interpretations about test subjects should, therefore, be placed on idiographic content analysis. The shaky psychometric foundations of the traditional perceptual categories suggest that quantitative evaluation of the Rorschach record must play a complementary, rather than a primary, role in clinical Rorschach work. It is within this conceptual framework that the present text is designed to educate.

A RORSCHACH INTRODUCTION
Content and Perceptual Approaches

Test Administration and Blot Characteristics

TEST ADMINISTRATION

Materials

Only a few materials are necessary for the Rorschach test.

1. The Rorschach blots. A reasonably new set of blots should be used. The examiner should avoid using smudged or otherwise damaged inkblots.
2. Stopwatch. A stopwatch that is calibrated to seconds is desirable for purposes of calculating the reaction time to each blot.
3. Recording paper. Blank 8½″ × 11″ paper—5–15 sheets for each testing will be necessary, depending on the length of the record and the recording style of the examiner. The examiner may wish to use a clipboard for holding the recording sheets.
4. Test forms. One or two location sheets, one summary sheet, and one tabulation sheet (see Chapter 5) will be necessary for each testing.

Setting

Testing should be done in a comfortable, well-lighted room. The examiner should ensure that interruptions and distractions (e.g., a telephone ringing, someone knocking on the door, etc.) will not interfere with the test session.

There is some controversy among psychologists as to the proper seating arrangement for Rorschach testing. Some psychologists prefer sitting to the right or left, slightly behind the subject, analogous to a psychoanalytic psychotherapy session. The present authors prefer sitting in a natural fashion at a desk with the subject at the corner. This has the advantage of not differentiating the Rorschach test from other tests in the battery (intelligence test, etc.), thus avoiding the arousal of undue anxiety in the subject. This arrangement also prevents the desk being used as a barrier between examiner and subject (Fig. 1-1).

The blots are kept face down in a pile in front of the examiner, with Card I on top. The completed blots are also kept face down, with the subject placing them in the face-down position after the responses to the blot are obtained.

Rapport Considerations

The attitude the subject has about the testing is important and can have a strong influence on the quality of the test responses. If a subject perceives the testing to be threatening or a waste of time, this will have a detrimental effect on what is elicited. It is vital, therefore, that the subject understand the purpose of the testing, as far as is possible or practical.

It is often helpful to first ask the subject how he or she felt about coming for the test session. This question can be used as a lead-in to a discussion of the subject's feelings regarding the testing and his or her understanding of its purpose. Distortions in the subject's understanding of the testing can then be corrected, and the subject can be told, in a very general or more specific manner, how the testing will be helpful to him or her.

This discussion with the subject must, of course, be conducted with discretion. If a subject is referred for testing because a therapist suspects a possible underlying psychosis, for example, it would be quite inappropriate for the examiner to impart this information. Often, a very general explanation will suffice: "In order for us to help you, we would first like to know as much about you as we can."

It is important that the Rorschach test in particular, and projective tests in general, not be regarded as procedures in which the subject can be treated in a detached, mechanical, and rigid manner and "tested." While standardization of administration is important with the Rorschach test, the nature and quality of the relationship between the examiner and the subject are also important. It is vital that the subject experience the examiner as a helping party, someone to be trusted. Establishing such a "set" in the test subject is,

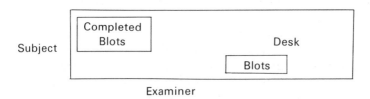

Figure 1-1. Proper seating arrangement for Rorschach testing.

therefore, an important part of the testing in general and the pre-test conversation in particular (Leventhal, Slepian, Gluck, & Rosenblatt, 1962).

There are subjects, however, who remain resistive to and suspicious of testing despite the efforts of the examiner. Testing should not necessarily be abandoned under such circumstances, but it should be recognized that the subject will likely be minimally productive on the Rorschach and other projective tests.

Administration of the Rorschach Test

Traditional Rorschach administration procedure involves two distinct phases of the test: the *Association phase*, in which the subject states what he or she sees in the blots, and the *Inquiry phase*, in which the examiner asks clarifying questions about the subject's responses. As will be discussed in a subsequent chapter, the examiner may wish to substitute a *Content Inquiry* for the more traditional type of inquiry. Furthermore, some examiners also use a third phase of testing, usually called *Testing-the-Limits*. This will be discussed later in this chapter. The present discussion will focus on the two traditional phases of Rorschach testing, Association and Inquiry.

Association Phase

In the Association phase of testing, the subject is asked to state what he or she sees on all 10 blots. It is often helpful for neophyte testers to prepare a $5'' \times 8''$ index card with the Association and Inquiry instructions and questions written on the two sides of the card. This instruction card can then be kept with the Rorschach blots.

The test instructions that precede the Association phase should be as follows:

> I'm going to show you 10 inkblots, and I would like you to tell me what each inkblot looks like or resembles. They are not designed to look like anything in particular, so there are no right or wrong answers. Different people see different things. Now, what does this first blot look like to you?

The first blot is then handed in an upright position to the subject. It is frequently useful to encourage the subject to hold the blot in his or her hand— this seems to bring about a more active involvement on the part of the subject. If the subject is resistant to doing so, however, it is not necessary to insist.

Subjects will sometimes ask questions in an attempt to get the examiner to further structure the situation for them: e.g., "How many things should I see?" "Can I turn the card?," etc. The response to such questions should be an indication that these decisions are up to the subject—e.g., "That's entirely up to you," etc.

Timing is begun as soon as the blot is presented to the subject. The reaction time is recorded when the subject begins verbalizing *a scorable response*. Thus, if the subject makes a comment such as, "It doesn't look like much to me," timing continues since this is not a scorable response. If the subject then states, "It could be a bat," the timing should cease with the first word of this sentence. The notion of a scorable response will be developed further in Chapter 2.

The examiner should try to record all responses *verbatim*, including side comments. Although this will be difficult for novice examiners, use of a shorthand method of recording, as discussed later in this chapter, is helpful. We do not favor tape recording of responses by the novice examiner as a substitute for the written record. Tape recording Rorschach responses greatly increases the length of time required for testing because all tapes must be transcribed, nor does it help the examiner learn the skill of writing down the patient's comments verbatim. In the long run, the examiner usually will need to learn this anyway.

If the subject speaks too quickly for the examiner to record responses verbatim, the subject may be asked to speak more slowly, or the last few words that the subject has spoken may be repeated by the examiner while he or she records them. Such "slowing down" of the subject should be done sparingly, however, so as not to unduly affect the spontaneity of the test situation.

If the subject gives only one response to Card I and indicates that he or she is finished with the blot, the examiner should then say to the subject: "Some people see more than one thing. Do you see anything else?" It should be noted that this is *only* done with Card I. If more responses then follow, the examiner should continue to record them. If the patient indicates that nothing further is seen, this should be accepted. Generally, a maximum of six responses per card is sufficient. Beyond this number, a subject is likely to be repetitious and/or overly immersed in minor details of the blots. As a rule of thumb, therefore, we will stop the subject if he or she is continuing to give responses to a blot after already having offered six.

Following completion of the subject's responses to Card I, Cards II through X are presented to the subject. As each card is given to the testee, it is useful to make comments such as: "and what might this blot look like or resemble?" The presentation of the blots should be done in a relaxed and comfortable rather than a stilted and rigid manner, in keeping with the very clinical nature of the Rorschach test.

Inquiry Phase

Following the completion of the subject's responses to the 10 blots, the Inquiry phase of testing begins. The purpose of the Inquiry phase is to make the scoring of the traditional Rorschach categories—location, determinants, content, populars, and form-level—possible (see Chapters 2, 3, and 4).

The instructions used with the Inquiry phase begin as follows:

> There is one more part to this test. I'm going to go through your responses with you, and I would like you to tell me where you saw the various things that you mentioned and what about the blots made them look like that to you. Now, on the first blot (blot shown to the subject) you saw _____. Please circle on this location sheet where you saw it.

This essentially constitutes the first question of the Inquiry phase, i.e., with respect to location. On subsequent responses during the inquiry, the examiner also repeats the subject's responses from the Association phase.

The subject will circle his or her percept on the location sheet. The examiner should then label the circled percept with the appropriate number— 1, 2, etc. If many overlapping responses to the same blot might make the location sheet difficult to decipher, a second location sheet should be used.

Sometimes subjects will misunderstand and try to circle the percept on the blot itself. The examiner should be alert to this possibility and stop the subject before the blot is damaged. The examiner may also wish to ask the subject to label parts of the response (e.g., wings, head, body, etc. of the bat), particularly if it is an atypical percept or if it is difficult for the examiner to perceive it in the blot.

Once the location of a percept is ascertained, the inquiry then turns to the question of determinants. At this point, the examiner wishes to know whether the shape, the color, and/or the shading of the blots helped to determine the response, and whether movement is perceived. It should be noted that movement is the one determinant that derives essentially from the subject's imagination, in contrast to form, color, and shading which are actual elements of the stimulus that the individual chooses to utilize or ignore. The examiner might, thus, introduce this part of the inquiry on a particular percept with a question such as: "What on the blot suggested _____ to you?" However, there is no standard set of inquiry questions.

The purpose of the inquiry is to enable the examiner to score the test protocol. Thus, if the determinants of the response are clear from the Association phase of testing, for example, there may be no need to pursue determinants in the inquiry. The simple repeating of the subject's response as a stimulus often produces verbalizations from the subject that are sufficient for scoring purposes. This is particularly the case as the inquiry progresses, and the subject understands the general direction of the inquiry.

If the examiner deems it necessary to probe for the presence of movement in connection with a percept, the examiner may wish to ask the subject to "tell me how you see (the bat)?" The examiner may sometimes ask how the subject sees the arms or legs of a figure if movement is suspected as a possible determinant.

At times, the examiner may also wish to probe very generally for further information relevant to scoring—asking, for example, "Tell me more about (the bat) you saw."

An important point is that when inquiring as to determinants, the examiner must be careful *not* to directly indicate the relevant determinants. Thus, it is incorrect to ask such questions as: "Does the color of the blot make it look like _____ to you?" or "Do you see it moving?" However, more subtle aids in the inquiry are possible. Thus, if chromatic color is suspected as a possible determinant, the examiner may ask the subject if the same percept is seen on the (achromatic) location sheet. If it isn't, then color may be assumed to be a determinant of the response, even though it was not stated by the test subject.

The examiner must also avoid asking such questions as: "Why do you see (a bat)?" Such questions call upon the subject to *justify* his or her response. It should be clear at all times that the examiner accepts the subject's responses and is merely seeking further information about them.

A perusal of the material on determinants (see Chapter 3) will probably be necessary at this point in order for the examiner to conduct an adequate determinant inquiry. Once the inquiry is completed for all of the responses, the standard Rorschach test administration is completed. It should be noted that subjects will sometimes give further responses during the Inquiry phase (i.e., perceive more percepts) that were not perceived during the Association phase. If this occurs, these responses (called additional responses), are also recorded and an Inquiry carried out if necessary for scoring. The distinction between main and additional responses will be discussed in subsequent chapters on scoring.

Testing-the-Limits

The Testing-the-Limits procedure is sometimes used by the examiner to explore the extent to which the subject is *capable* of giving certain categories of response which are largely absent from the test record. For example, if there is a dearth of popular responses or of whole responses in the test record, is the subject nonetheless able to perceive whole or popular responses? A further question answered in the Testing-the-Limits procedure is how much leading on the part of the examiner is necessary in order to elicit such a response from the subject.

When using this optional procedure after the Association and Inquiry phases have been completed, the examiner again presents certain Rorschach blots to the test subject, beginning with very general questions. If there is an absence of whole responses in the test record, for example, the examiner may present blots which lend themselves readily to whole responses, such as

Cards IV and V. A general question might then be asked, such as: "Sometimes, people use all of the blot in seeing things—can you do that?" The subject's responses are then observed and recorded, thereby indicating whether he or she is *capable* of using the inkblots in this manner. If the subject cannot respond with a whole response at this juncture, questioning might then become more specific—suggesting a common percept, e.g., a bat on Card V. If the subject is still unable to see such a percept, the examiner might then point out specific part of the percept (the wings, the head, etc.). The degree of aid required by the subject naturally constitutes very relevant information regarding the subject's capacities and orientation.

Recording the Rorschach Responses

The paper used to record the Rorschach test performance is simply $8\frac{1}{2}'' \times 11''$ paper turned sideways. The paper is then divided into four columns. The first column is narrow and used to record card numbers, response numbers, and reaction times. The second and third columns are wide and are used to record the Association and Inquiry verbalizations, respectively. The last column is narrow and is used for scoring the responses. (See Fig. 1-2 and sample protocols in Chapter 12 for examples of our response forms.)

The examiner should try to line up each response in the Association phase with the corresponding Inquiry questions and answers. It is preferable to use one page for each inkblot, thus five pages and the backs of those pages are used for the full test. Of course, further pages may be used if necessary. Roman numerals are used to represent the blot numbers, with Arabic numerals representing the response number on each blot. We use the lower-case letters (a), (b), (c), and (d) to represent the examiner asking the four most common types of inquiry questions, pertaining respectively to location (a), determinants in general (b), movement in particular (c), and the more general probing type of question (e.g., "tell me more about (the bat)," (d). Other questions and comments the examiner makes should also be recorded in parentheses. We use the notation (> 1) to represent the examiner telling the subject on the first blot that some people see more than one thing. If the blot is not upright when a response is given, the position in which the subject is holding the blot is indicated by a carat ($\vee$, $<$, or $>$), with the point indicating the location of the top of the card. If the subject turns the card around, this is indicated by an arrow ⊚. If additional responses occur, these are labeled A1, A2, etc. for each blot.

The recording paper for Card I responses for a hypothetical subject might resemble Fig. 1-2.

I.5″	1.	It ll a bat	1. (a) Just the whole thing. (b) The wings and the black color.	W	FM	A	+ P
	2.	It also cd be a woman in the middle, doing a dance. She has on a transparent dress.	2. (a)	D	M	H	+ P
	3.	V I also c 2 animals moving around.	3. They're at the side, w their mouths open. (b) Just the shapes and posture.	D	FM	A	+
			A1. I also c 2 people w wings, holding onto st in the middle.	W	M	(H)	+
			Here they are. (b) These r the people—they just ll it. (d) They might be pulling on the thing in the middle.				

Figure 1-2. Sample recording sheet for Card I.

This subject gave one response to the first blot, then gave two more after being told that some people see more than one thing. The card was rotated 360 degrees prior to the second response; the third response was with the card in an inverted position. In the second response, the subject gave sufficient information in the Association phase (with reference to transparency shading and movement) so that further inquiry was superfluous. The subject gave one additional response on Card I, which was then inquired for. In both the third and the additional responses, the location of the response was clear; no location question was asked. For the additional response, the examiner chose to ask a further probing question: "Tell me more about the people with wings." The fourth column is used for scoring (see Chapters 2, 3, and 4).

It should be noted that the responses to Cards II through X would be labeled, 1, 2, 3, etc., as they were on Card I.

To aid in recording verbalizations quickly, the examiner should begin to use a shorthand manner of recording, particularly for commonly occurring expressions. The abbreviations should not be too extensive or too difficult for someone else to decipher, however, since another psychologist may wish to look over the test protocol at a future time. Some commonly used abbreviations are shown in Table 1-1.

Table 1-1
Commonly Used Abbreviations

ll = looks like	bec = because
DK = don't know	et = everything
bf = butterfly	wd = would
cd = could	r = are
w = with	c = see
st = something	u = you
so = someone	

Testing Children

Some special considerations are made in the administration procedures when the subject is a child. In the previous literature on this subject, however, substantial disagreement has existed on exactly what should be altered in the administration of the Rorschach with child subjects. On the one hand, Klopfer et al. (1956) state that: "In our clinical experience, we have never encountered the need to depart from the standard administrative procedure, except to gear the language to the level of the child's comprehension" (p. 14).

On the other hand, there are those who advocate specific modifications with child subjects, e.g., use of a trial blot before the regular series (Hertz, 1936), avoiding the recording of reaction time (Halpern, 1953), use of an immediate inquiry (Francis-Williams, 1968; Halpern, 1960), and greater emphasis on establishing rapport, even to the extent of having the small child subject sit on the examiner's lap (Halpern, 1953).

Our experience has shown that the Rorschach test should not be administered to subjects under the age of 5 (though a very mature 4-year-old might still be a test subject). It is also recommended that the examiner be even more concerned about establishing rapport and encouraging the child than would be the case with an adult subject. Thus, as always with the Rorschach test, the goal should be seen as the garnering of important information about the test subject. One should not strive for a barren and counterproductive "standardization" which essentially produces a Rorschach record of little or no clinical use. This is particularly the case with young children.

We do not use a sample inkblot, but when using the traditional administration and scoring technique for children aged 5–8, we do recommend immediate inquiry for determinants, etc., after each inkblot rather than in a separate inquiry phase. We typically do not have even the very young child sit on our laps, but try to relate to him or her in as warm, encouraging, and flexible a manner as possible (e.g., taking a break, if necessary, during the test administration). Generally, we are more willing to compromise standardization in favor of rapport with very young and with immature children.

THE RORSCHACH BLOTS

Hermann Rorschach's initial experimentation was done with 15 ink-blots, but he was only able to have his work printed by agreeing to limit the test to 10. The printer reduced Rorschach's blots in size, altered their colors, and through defects in printing, also introduced varieties of shading not intended by the author (Ellenberger, 1954). These altered and imperfect reproductions of Rorschach's plates constitute what are known today throughout the world as the Rorschach test.

Rorschach students should acquaint themselves with the stimulus value of the 10 blots, since in the process of interpreting a protocol, the examiner must constantly seek to disentangle the stimulus-determined parts of the protocol from parts that represent dynamic projections of the subject's personality. As Zubin (1956) notes: "Some responses reflect more heavily the stimulus properties; others reflect these to a lesser degree, and the latter are called 'projective'" (p. 183).

The 10 blots of the Rorschach test are divided into the five achromatic or black-and-white cards (Cards I, IV, V, VI, and VII) and the five chromatic or colored cards (Cards II, III, VIII, IX, and X). Of the chromatic series, Cards II and III are printed in black and red; Cards VIII, IX, and X are printed in a variety of bright colors.

The Ten Blots

Card I

The research literature dealing with responses to Card I generally supports the common-sense clinical view that the subject is presented with a stressful new situation. It has been our observation that in response to the first Rorschach blot, the subject often reveals a great deal about his or her personality. It is, so to speak, the subject's first chance on the test to tell you who he or she is.

The literature also supports the notion that Card I is perceived quite negatively and has a negative stimulus value that is second only to Card IV. Negatively toned responses to Card I must, therefore, be interpreted with a great deal of caution. Responses such as "a rather ugly bat" or "a sinister-looking moth" may simply be appropriate reactions to the stimulus properties of Card I.

Card II

In general, the literature suggests that this blot tends to be upsetting to certain classes of subjects, the chromatic color being largely responsible. Females tend to report dislike of Card II in particular, perhaps, as suggested by Hershenson (1949), due to an association with menstrual blood. Some research also indicates more reactions of dislike to this blot among unstable rather than stable subjects.

Clinicians generally cite Card II as sexually evocative (with a penis area near the top and a vaginal area beneath). This was corroborated in a study by Pascal, Roesch, Devine, and Suttell (1950), in which Card II was found to be the second most evocative blot for sexual responses.

Card III

Many clinicians place great stock in responses to Card III as an indication of social interaction patterns. Thus, if popular human figures are seen on this blot, are they described as engaged in a cooperative action, a battle, etc.? Unfortunately, no convincing empirical data relevant to this assertion about Card III have been presented.

Clinicians have also stated that the absence of human association on this card should be considered pathological (e.g., Allen, 1966). Data presented by Hammer (1966), however, indicate that a surprisingly large number of normal subjects do not report seeing people on this blot (23 percent of normal females, 27 percent of normal males).

The sexes of the figures perceived on this blot have also been of interest to clinicians. The simplest (and unfortunately, a very persistent) interpretation in this regard is to see the sex of the figure as indicative of the sexual identification of the subject. Thus, a male subject who sees female figures might be viewed as having a feminine sexual identification. Given the large percentages of subjects reported by Ames (1975) who perceived figures of the opposite sex on Card III, such simplistic interpretation of sexual identification is clearly unwarranted.

In our experience, the gender characteristics of Card III do constitute highly useful clinical material. This is especially true in cases where the subject is perplexed and disturbed over the possible sex of the figures, and is either unable to reach a decision, or describes the figures as having both male and female sexual parts. Such responses often indicate confused sexual identification.

Card IV

Many clinicians believe that Card IV tends to elicit feelings towards the father and, hence, this blot has often been referred to as the "father card." Empirical studies on this point have yielded equivocal results, suggesting that such an interpretation of Card IV responses may be incorrect.

The problem is compounded by the clear and consistent negative image of Card IV. This blot elicits fewer positive responses than any of the other blots. Such negatively-toned responses as "a large ugly animal" or "a frightening gorilla" may thus be appropriate responses to the stimulus characteristics of the blot rather than a reflection of underlying dynamic trends. This leads to the frequent potential error noted by Zimmerman, Lambert, and Class (1966): "The strongly negative quality typically ascribed to [Card] IV suggest[s] an implicit bias . . . which might lead a naive examiner to find all his subjects obsessed with . . . negative attitudes toward authority" (p. 259).

It is our belief that Card IV can help elicit attitudes toward authority figures (whether male or female), but such interpretations should not be made without sufficient evidence, particularly regarding negative feelings toward male authority figures. Clinicians should also keep in mind that attitudes toward the father and authority in general may be projected on any of the blots.

Card V

This blot has been referred to as the "reality card" because of the ease with which it elicits the popular winged object. It is thought to be an easy card for the subject, relatively undisturbing, and to provide a breathing space after the disturbing character of the earlier cards. The research literature generally supports these views, indicating, for example, that this blot is the easiest on which to obtain a high form-level response. The blot has also been shown to draw the least number of sexual responses from subjects.

Some clinicians have suggested pathological implications for a failure to see the popular flying animal, but a study by Molish (1951) did not find this to differentiate between normal, neurotic, and schizophrenic groups. This type of interpretation must therefore be considered doubtful.

Card VI

This blot has been referred to as the "sex card" because of the phallic symbol at the top and a vaginal symbol below. Pascal et al. (1950) found that Card VI was the blot most frequently responded to with sexual percepts.

On the whole, the general empirical evidence on blot stimulus characteristics indicates that Card VI is sexually suggestive, particularly of male sexuality, and that it tends to elicit negative reactions. However, blanket interpretations should not be made on the assumption that this card is the so-called sex card. The clinician should be aware that information relevant to sexual functioning can be brought forth by other blots. Furthermore, it must be recognized that it is difficult for subjects to see clear percepts on Card VI, which also affects subjects' responses to this blot.

Card VII

Card VII traditionally has been regarded by clinicians as the reverse of Card IV; subjects are thought to respond positively to the blot and concepts appropriate to a mother-child relationship are thought to be involved. Thus, Card VII has been referred to as the "mother card."

Research data indicate that Card VII often elicits a positive response from subjects, but the evidence of this card's particular ability to evoke attitudes toward the mother is not encouraging. Card VII is also one of the most difficult blots in terms of producing responses of good form-level.

Clinicians should be aware that attitudes toward the mother can be projected onto any card, and should be wary of categorically interpreting Card VII responses in terms of the mother without sufficient evidence. In view of the predominantly female gender of sexual responses to this card, it also seems likely that some subjects can be expected to react to the female genitals perceived on the blot.

Card VIII

Clinicians have generally asserted that Card VIII can be considered a mild stimulus, given the soft pastel coloring and the ease of discerning animals at the side. Other interpretations include the suggestion that failure to perceive the popular animals should be considered indicative of serious disturbance, and the suggestion that the type of animal seen should be considered an expression of certain ego qualities.

The empirical data definitely suggest that Card VIII is one of the most preferred blots and that the colors add to the generally positive response. Normal subjects have been shown to give the popular animal response more frequently than schizophrenics (Molish, 1951). There are as yet no data relevant to the "ego qualities" hypothesis as to the type of animal seen.

It is suggested that clinicians refrain from interpreting the very popular animals (bears, rodents) that are often seen in response to the blot in the absence of evidence that the specific animal has some dynamic meaning for the subject. It is also advisable that clinicians investigate the testee's associations to the specific types of animals seen, because although the choice of animal may indeed have dynamic significance, the meaning may be idiosyncratic to the test subject (see Chapter 7).

Card IX

Both the clinical and the research literature on this blot agree that Card IX has an unstructured quality that makes it difficult to discern percepts. This blot is consequently the most frequently rejected, has the slowest reaction time of the 10 blots, and is the most difficult on which to produce percepts of good form-level. This blot also usually elicits a positive response, which is augmented by the color of the blot. However, neurotic subjects generally respond less positively to this blot than do normal subjects. As noted by Klopfer and Davidson (1962), this blot elicits a great variety of responses, thus adding to its value in the Rorschach series.

Card X

Card X is a complex blot and somewhat disorganized. The coloring yields a positive response from subjects, but the lack of cohesiveness often elicits a negative reaction. Card X has been judged the second most difficult blot on which to distinguish percepts. It also has one of the slowest reaction times and is second only to Card IX in terms of the difficulty of producing high form-level responses.

In our experience and in the opinions of Alcock (1963) and Halpern (1953), key dynamic responses are often elicited on Card X because it is the last in the series. "The note on which the subject is willing to let the matter rest is of great importance, frequently representing a composite picture of his problems and conflict" (Halpern, 1953, p. 52). On Card X, the subject has his or her last opportunity to tell the examiner who he or she is.

OVERVIEW

Each of the 10 Rorschach blots is a distinct stimulus that influences responses. In the process of test interpretation, the examiner must strive to untangle the stimulus elements from the dynamic elements in each subject's responses, as well as possible interactions between the two. In interpreting the Rorschach protocols, the following general guidelines are suggested: the examiner should be most reluctant to accord dynamic meaning to those responses that are in keeping with the stimulus qualities of the blots, and should conversely give greater weight to those responses that seem out of step with the blot stimulus characteristics.

The examiner should be warned against making blanket assumptions regarding Card IV as the "father card," Card VI as the "sex card," Card VII as the "mother card," etc. Because the dynamic referents of many Rorschach responses are unclear, it would be of great practical help to the Rorschach clinician if such assumptions could be made. However, the research data do not generally support such blanket assumptions about card meaning. The clinician faced with obscure responses and symbols in the patient's test record would do better to clarify the dynamic meaning of the responses through the techniques presented in Chapter 9.

2

Defining the Response
and Scoring for Location

Fundamentally, the Rorschach may be regarded as both a standardized interview and as a behavioral sample of the subject's perceptual operations, in a situation using standardized, but comparatively unstructured stimuli. Once such information about the subject is obtained, the examiner is confronted with the task of classifying and organizing these data so that they will lend themselves to meaningful personality interpretation. The assumption implicit in Rorschach testing is that the subject's associations to the blots are very much like his or her typical perceptions outside of the examination situation. The ambiguity of the inkblots, however, makes it far more difficult for subjects to draw upon conventional response patterns and well-practiced behaviors. Thus, a great deal is revealed about the subject's adaptive maneuvers and aspects of his or her personality which are frequently disguised in the ordinary course of everyday living.

The Rorschach scoring process is basically an attempt to provide a summary of the subject's performance; it utilizes a kind of symbolic shorthand that enables various components of perception and association and their interrelationships to be quantified. The sets of scoring rules developed for the Rorschach provide a commonly understood communication network for Rorschach workers and also facilitate the comparison of a particular subject's protocol with Rorschach data available for a broad spectrum of groups identified on the basis of numerous criteria. Scoring can, therefore, be seen as an important step in making the subject's productions more manageable for evaluation.

THE SCORING CATEGORIES—AN OVERVIEW

The approach to scoring used here is essentially that of Klopfer and his associates. Based on the clinical, research, and teaching experience of the authors, however, the Klopfer system has been modified where it was felt to be too complex and/or somewhat arbitrary.

Every Rorschach percept is scored from five different standpoints. First, the location score encompasses where the percept was seen and how much of the blot was incorporated in the concept.

A second element scored, called determinants, entails a consideration of the qualities of the inkblot that determine how the percept was seen. Determinants are classed as form, movement, color, and shading.

The third category is scoring each response for one of a wide range of content possibilities that reflect the subject matter of the percept.

The fourth score assigned is for form level, which taps the accuracy of the percept in terms of congruence between shape of the blot area chosen and the configuration of the concept seen. Put another way, form level assesses whether a reasonable "fit" exists between the inkblot and the response.

The fifth and last scoring category involves the degree of conventionality of the percept. If a percept is very commonly seen, it is labeled a popular. If, on the other hand, it occurs only once in 100 records, it is designated original. It should be noted that the great majority of responses are neither popular nor original.

In addition to the five major scoring categories, an effort is made to indicate various qualitative aspects of the subject's performance. This includes such aspects as distorted thinking manifested in responses that combine realistically incompatible percepts as, for example, on Card V: "the whole thing is a bat with human legs coming out of the wings."

THE SCORABLE RESPONSE

Before embarking on a formal scoring procedure, it must be ascertained what can be legitimately scored. This is not always an easy matter because a response, per se, may not be sufficiently differentiated from a comment or remark. This may be particularly apparent in the case of young children and, to a lesser degree, in adults with limited verbal ability. As far as possible, all verbalizations should be recorded regardless of whether they are judged to be a remark or, subsequently, a legitimate response. An emotionally charged comment appended to a scorable percept can sometimes be far more revealing than the percept as such, especially if the latter turns out to be a vague, poorly defined concept.

A response is a separate, discrete idea or concept given in association to a clearly delineated portion of the blot or to the entire inkblot. It is sometimes necessary to question the subject quite directly with respect to whether the association was intended as a remark or a response. If the subject states it was meant as a response and an elabortion or further explanation is offered, then it is generally scored as a response.

One of the most difficult aspects of traditional Rorschach scoring is the differentiation between a *specification* and a *separate response*. In general, one should be guided by two principles in distinguishing a specification from a response: (1) the tightness or looseness with which the total concept is described (the more tightly bound the concept, the less likely the scorer should be to assign more than one response to it) and (2) whether or not elements of the concept can be and commonly are seen by themselves. Examples are given in the following three verbalizations:

Card II:	It looks like two people with hats on their heads.
Card III:	I see two men pulling apart a crab.
Card X:	An underwater sea scene—crabs up here, sea urchins, and seahorses.

The verbalization to Card II is a tightly organized response; furthermore, the hat, while not an uncommon response to the top red area, is really a specification of the head of the figure seen. Thus, only one response would be scored for Card II. The Card III verbalization, however, while still fairly tightly organized, contains an element (the crab) very often perceived as a separate response by subjects. Thus, two responses would be scored on Card III. The verbalization to Card X is clearly four separate responses, since the concept is both loosely organized and contains elements often perceived as separate responses. (The sets of responses to both Cards III and X should be bracketed, as described below.)

Klopfer proposes two broad scoring categories of responses: main and additional. In our experience, however, the distinction between these two classifications is often rather confusing. Consequently, this aspect of Klopfer scoring has been revised under the present scoring system: *Main responses* are only those percepts given spontaneously during the initial phase of the test or in what is termed the performance proper. *The additional* scoring category is reserved entirely for new concepts given during the inquiry phase of the test, or for associations offered during the performance proper and then rejected in the course of the inquiry. Clarifications, elaborations, or further ideas elicited during the inquiry phase to percepts already reported during the spontaneous association phase of testing are still included under main responses and are scored through the use of multiple determinants.

In the Klopfer system, a main response receives only one location, form level, determinant, content, and popularity-originality score. By contrast, in our approach, a percept may be scored for several location, determinant, and content categories that are not differentiated on the basis of being primary or secondary. As will be discussed in the section on tabulation, eliminating the notion of single main determinant scoring clearly results in a far more inclusive and meaningful scoring system. It also obviates the need of applying arbitrary rules of precedence when making a main determinant assignment. For example, if a subject responded to the center red area of Card III as "a beautiful butterfly in flight," and went on to explain in the course of the inquiry that it appeared to look like a butterfly because of the attractive color and the graceful movement of its wings, it would be necessary under the Klopfer main-additional scoring system to decide whether movement or color was the main determinant. The other determinant, though perhaps of very nearly equal importance to the percept, would be designated as an additional and would not figure in the computations of any of the ratios and percentages.

LOCATION

Although it seems a simple matter to have the subject indicate where in the particular inkblot he or she saw the percept, this is often not the case. A number of subjects are defensively evasive and exceedingly vague in their percepts. The reverse is true also—some subjects are inordinately precise and insist on excluding many minute sections of the blots from their associations. A location sheet of the 10 blots reproduced in miniature is certainly a great help in fixing the boundaries of the blot areas used in the percept. However, many subjects, when asked to outline their percepts on a location sheet, do not invest a great deal in this assignment and are only perfunctory in their performance.

Because certain types of responses recur over and over again in particular blot areas, it is extremely helpful in scoring if the examiner takes the time initially to become familiar with the specific blot areas and responses ordinarily found in such areas. One way this can be achieved is by utilizing a comprehensive breakdown of areas such as that compiled by Hertz (1970) in her book, *Frequency Tables for Scoring Rorschach Responses*. Students who study the Hertz card diagrams and frequency tables (with a set of the Rorschach plates in front of them to see the percepts more clearly) will feel far more at ease and confident in their location scoring.

As previously mentioned, location refers to the part of the blot that was utilized in the formation of the percept. Essentially, location responses may be divided into wholes and various categories of detail responses.

Whole Responses, W, W̶, and DW

In the category of whole responses, scored W, the entire blot is used with the exception of the white space; or it is obvious that the subject fully intended to use the whole blot but may have accidentally omitted a small area. Examples of whole responses are as follows:

Card I:	It resembles a bat. The whole thing. It has its wings spread.
Card VI (upside down):	The entire dark area looks like two Russian dancers with cossack hats.

In cut-off whole, or W̶, percepts, the subject uses minimally two-thirds of the blot and indicates that his or her intent was to use as much of the blot as possible with the conceivable exception of some comparatively small areas. Examples of W̶ responses include:

Card V:	This is a moth but these (side extentions) don't belong.
Card VI:	Looks like a bear skin rug but the very top is not part of it.

A confabulatory whole, DW, is scored when a subject selects a small portion of the blot and then proceeds to give a whole response, justifying it on the basis of the small detail even when the concept is at variance with the configuration of the blot. By definition, a DW response is always poor form and represents an over-generalization that is incongruous with the blot shape. Two graphic examples of DW responses follow:

Card VIII:	The center looks like a spine and the rest must therefore be body organs.
Card X:	It must be the buildings of Paris because the center looks like the Eiffel Tower.

Usual Detail Responses: D and d

When a comparatively large section of the blot is used for the subject's concept and is readily delineated by space, color, or shading from the remainder of the blot, it is scored a large usual detail, D. A substantially smaller area that is just as easily demarcated in the blot is labled a small usual detail with a d scoring. Designating these locations as "usual" conveys that they are the more obvious and frequently used portions of the blots. A list of these large and small usual details areas for each Rorschach card with the various areas actually outlined on miniature inkblots is reproduced from

Klopfer, Klopfer, Ainsworth, and Holt (1954), with their permission. It should also be noted that simple combinations of D and d areas would also be scored respectively as D or d; e.g., "a pig" seen on the bottom two-thirds of one side of Card VII would be scored D. The large and small usual detail areas of the 10 inkblots are reproduced on the following pages.

Card I

Large Usual Details

D_1 Entire center with or without lighter gray in lower portion.

D_2 Entire side.

D_3 Lower center without lighter gray.

D_4 Entire lower center.

D_5 Upper side.

D_6 Upper third of center.

Small Usual Details

d_1 Upper outer projections.

d_2 Lower side.

d_3 Upper, inner, claw-like extensions.

d_4 Uppermost projections.

d_5 Upper innermost details.

d_6 Bottom projection.

d_7 Small knob-like extension at lower side.

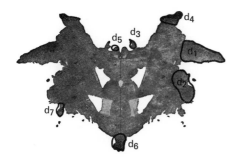

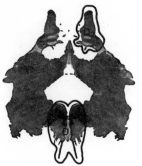

Card II

Large Usual Details

D_1 Lower red with or without black-red mixture.

D_2 Upper red.

D_3 Entire side black.

D_4 Upper portion of black.

Small Usual Details

d_1 Upper center.

d_2 Bottom outer projection.

d_3 Bottom projection adjacent to preceding *d*.

d_4 Upper side projection.

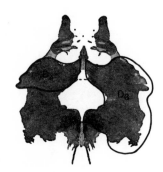

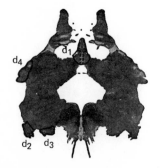

Card III

Large Usual Details

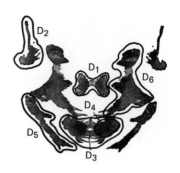

D_1 Inner red.

D_2 Outer red with or without tail-like extension.

D_3 Entire lower center.

D_4 Lower center black.

D_5 Lower side black.

D_6 Upper side black, head and upper part of body of usual figure.

D_7 Middle side black.

D_8 One of the two human figures.

D_9 Lower center light gray.

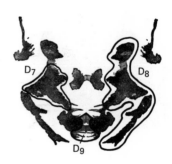

Small Usual Details

d_1 Bottom side portion, with or without lower part of "leg."

d_2 Top side black.

d_3 Side black lateral protrusion, usually upside down.

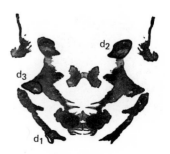

Card IV

Large Usual Details

D_1 Lower center.

D_2 Lower side black and gray, sometimes including upper side portion.

D_3 Lower side light gray.

D_4 Entire vertical dark center.

D_5 Inner dark side detail.

Small Usual Details

d_1 Upper side extensions, sometimes with small adjacent portion.

d_2 Uppermost portion, sometimes including adjacent shaded portion.

d_3 Outermost lower side extension.

d_4 Lowermost portion of lower center detail.

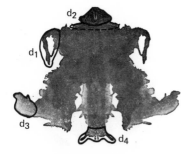

Card V

Large Usual Details

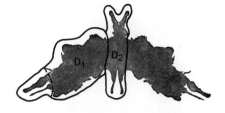

D₁   Entire side with or without light gray extensions.

D₂   Center vertical portion.

Small Usual Details

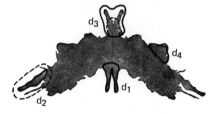

d₁   Bottom center.

d₂   Side extension sometimes with adjacent thin extension.

d₃   Top center, with or without uppermost protrusions.

d₄   Contour of upper side detail.

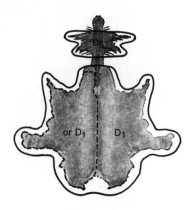

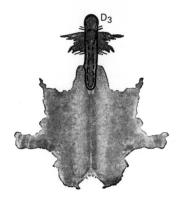

Card VI

Large Usual Details

D_1　Entire lower portion or half of lower portion.

D_2　Entire upper portion, sometimes including light gray uppermost portion of lower detail.

D_3　Upper black portion only of center column, sometimes without slightly shaded outer portion.

D_4　Entire dark vertical center.

D_5　Lighter part only of upper portion.

Small Usual Details

d_1　Uppermost detail with or without "whiskers."

d_2　Lower lateral extensions.

d_3　Two inner light gray ovals.

d_4　Bottom inner projections.

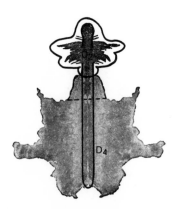

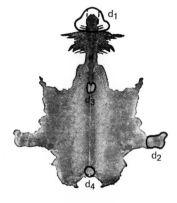

Card VII

Large Usual Details

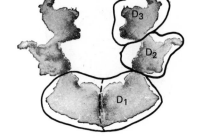

D_1 Entire bottom portion, sometimes each half separately.

D_2 Middle third.

D_3 Upper third, with or without uppermost projection.

D_4 Upper two-thirds.

Small Usual Details

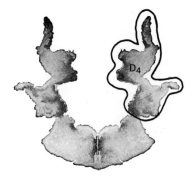

d_1 Dark center bottom detail.

d_2 Top projections.

d_3 Light gray projections on upper inner corner of top third.

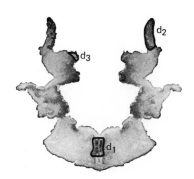

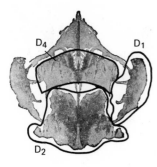

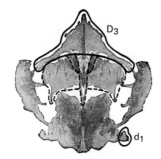

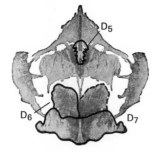

Card VIII

Large Usual Details

D_1 Side pink.

D_2 Lower pink and orange.

D_3 Top gray portion with or without center line, sometimes including rib-like figure and/or blue portion.

D_4 Middle blue portion.

D_5 Rib-like figure in upper center.

D_6 Bottom pink alone.

D_7 Bottom orange alone.

Small Usual Details

d_1 Lateral extensions of bottom orange.

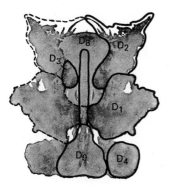 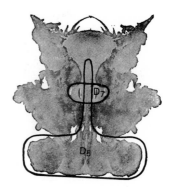

Card IX

Large Usual Details

D$_1$ Green portion.

D$_2$ Orange portion.

D$_3$ Small inner portion at junction of green and orange.

D$_4$ Lateral pink.

D$_5$ Entire pink portion plus center line, card inverted.

D$_6$ Entire pink or either half.

D$_7$ Center portion between lateral greens.

D$_8$ Center gray portion, with or without D$_7$.

D$_9$ Inner pink portion.

Small Usual Details

d$_1$ All or most of upper inner orange projections.

d$_2$ Eye-like portion in middle including green and white slits.

d$_3$ Arch-like light orange at top center.

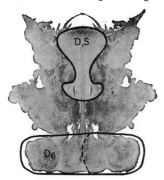 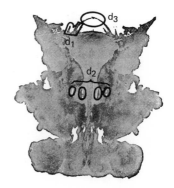

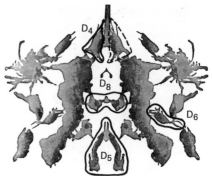

Card X

Large Usual Details

D₁   Outer blue, sometimes with outer green.

D₂   Inner green, dark portions only.

D₃   Entire gray portion at top.

D₄   Gray "animals" at top without inner gray column.

D₅   Entire inner green.

D₆   Outer gray-brown figures.

D₇   Light portion between inner greens.

D₈   Inner blue.

D₉   Pink portion separately.

D₁₀   Inner yellow.

D₁₁   Outer orange.

D₁₂   Inner orange.

D₁₃   Outer upper green.

D₁₄   Gray column at top without gray "animals" beside it.

D₁₅   Outer yellow.

D₁₆   Pink with entire top gray, card inverted.

D₁₇   Pink with inner blue.

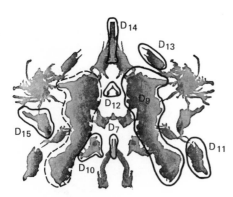
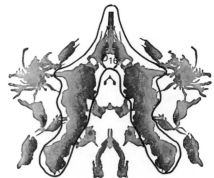

Unusual Details: dd, de, di, and dr

In contrast to the usual details, the unusual details are those percepts which cannot be classified as whole, usual details, or space responses. The symbol Dd is used to subsume all the types of percepts falling into this scoring category. It should be noted, however, that Dd is never employed to score an individual response. As the name implies, the unusual detail is not a commonplace area and occurs significantly less frequently than the usual detail.

The dd, or tiny detail response, alludes to percepts that occur in very small areas. The de detail denotes the use of only the contour or the very edge of the blot. If any other portion of the blot is used, the scoring is dd. The di, or inside detail, represents areas that are entirely within the inkblot and not easily differentiated by any of the obvious blot characteristics. The dr, or rare detail, refers to unusual locations that do not fall into any of the other usual or unusual scoring categories. These percepts often contain arbitrary subdivisions and/or omissions of a section of a very distinct blot area. They can be as small as the dd response or approach a W in size and can involve unusual combinations of usual detail percepts. Examples of the four types of unusual details and their locations are shown on page 32.

White Space Responses: S

A white space scoring depicts concepts that use the white area within a blot or surrounding it. It is essentially a reversal of figure and ground. Examples of white space responses are:

| Card II: | The white in the center looks like a space ship. |
| Card VII (upside down): | The middle reminds me of a bust of George Washington. |

White space can be combined with any of the other location scorings. For example:

| Card I: | A jack-o-lantern. These (the white spaces) are the eyes and the mouth. W (S) |
| Card I: | This is a huge ocean and these (little dots) are tiny islands. S (dd) |

For tabulation purposes there is really no difference between a response scored S (dd) or one scored dd (S). However, the parenthetical notation is useful to indicate whether the figure or ground seems primary in a

Examples of usual detail (Dd). *Tiny detail (dd)*: 1. Card I: A musical note; 2. Card III: Birds' beaks—they look sharp; 3. Card IX: A boot. *Edge detail (de)*: 4. Card V: An outline of a mountain; 5. Card VI: a man's profile; 6. Card X: A coastline. *Inner detail (di)*: 7. Card I: A target with the bullseye; 8. Card II: Kidney; 9. Card IX: Eyes. *Rare detail (dr)*: 10. Card IV: a chess piece—probably a pawn; 11. Card VII: A fish burying its nose into a mound of seaweed; 12. Card VIII: An animal face.

particular response; the location area that seems secondary is put in the parentheses.

Bracketing of Responses

In some situations, two or more separate responses may be related to one another. In such instances, the two or more location areas are bracketed. More specifically, bracketing of location scorings is often indicated when a subject first offers a detail response and then endeavors to include the remainder of the blot. This is typically done in somewhat indefinite fashion, for example:

Card VIII: Two animals of prey. The rest of the card could be woods, rocks, and water—hunting grounds.

These responses would be scored:

$$\left\{ \begin{array}{l} D \\ W \end{array} \right.$$

The bracketing indicates the relationship between these two responses.

The subject may also begin with a number of distinct detail responses on a particular card, and then endeavor to integrate the details by giving a casually organized whole percept. For example:

Card X: Crabs, seahorses, and coral. The whole thing must be an underwater scene.

These responses would be scored:

$$\left\{ \begin{array}{l} D \\ D \\ D \\ W \end{array} \right.$$

3

Scoring Determinants

As previously mentioned, determinant scores reflect the properties of the inkblot which contribute to the percept. The four principal categories are: form, movement, color, and shading. There may be one or a combination of determinants which are utilized in a particular response (see Chapter 1 for the inquiry technique to elicit determinants). In the case of multiple determinants, the one most important to the percept is listed first. Where it is impossible to ascertain the principal determinant, merely for convenience sake, the order of notation is: human movement, animal movement, color, and, lastly, shading. As indicated before, *all* determinants occurring in a multiple scoring are subsequently tabulated and appear in the various ratios found in the psychogram.

Practically speaking, multiple scoring ordinarily means a double determinant. On occasion, it may be necessary to have a triple determinant. Beyond three determinants, however, it is likely that the scoring process is best served by breaking the ostensible single percept into several separate responses which then may be bracketed to reflect their interrelationship. If the Rorschach scorer errs, it should be in the direction of parsimony rather than in the direction of overscoring.

FORM RESPONSES: F

When only the outline of the blot determines the response, the score given is F. This scoring is, in a sense, a scoring by exclusion: i.e., when movement, color, or shading are not elicited as determinants, leaving only the shape, F is scored. Form responses may have exceedingly vague contours, such as a map of an unspecified region or a rock. On the other hand, they may have a very definite shape, as, for example:

Card I (D4):	The liberty bell.
Card IV (D2):	Big boots.

As is the case for movement, color, and shading, F is not limited to any particular location area, but may be scored for percepts entailing any of the locations covered in Chapter 2.

MOVEMENT: M, FM, Fm, mF, and m

While form, color, and shading are present in various inkblots for subjects to utilize in their concepts if they so desire, it is obvious that incorporating movement into a response requires a subject to project some form of action or life. There are three principal types of movement percepts: human movement, animal movement, and inanimate movement. Human movement, M, is the appropriate scoring when the response indicates humanlike activity, expression, or posture. An M scoring may involve a whole human or a portion of a human figure in some form of action. The action may be very minimal, such as a facial expression. Furthermore, caricatures, statues, or animals which appear to be in humanlike action are also scored M. It is most important to recognize that implicit in all M percepts is a form dominant element, whether it be well-delineated or extremely vague. It is never correct, therefore, to score F separately from M for a given percept. Examples of various types of M responses are as follows:

Card III (W):	The whole thing reminds me of two people carrying something.
Card IV (W):	A giant, you can only see his huge shoes and legs, sitting on a stump.
Card VI (upper two-thirds):	Comic strip little old ladies glowering at each other.
Card II (Black area):	Two bears in love, kissing one another.

Paralleling human movement, FM is scored whenever animal-like action is present in a response. Such percepts may involve a whole or parts of an animal and drawings or caricatures of animals. Animals in humanlike activity receive an M scoring, but when animals are actually trained to perform like humans, such as a trained chimpanzee riding a bicycle, the appropriate scoring is FM rather than M. As was the case with M, form is also implied in FM responses and is never scored separately. Illustrations of FM percepts are:

Card I (W):	All of it looks like a bat, it has wings spread and seems to be flying.
Card VIII (W):	It reminds me of a fancy ornament, with the two sides resembling stalking leopards.
Card V (d_2):	The open jaws of a crocodile ready to receive its food.
Card II (D_2):	Two trained seals in a balancing act.

The inanimate movement category subsumes responses that convey the notion of natural or mechanical forces at work, forces which may at times be abstract or symbolic. In contrast to M and FM, inanimate movement has three subcategories which are utilized to differentiate between distinct form percepts, those which are semidefinite, and those which are entirely vague or indefinite. The Fm type of movement scoring is appropriate when there is a clear-cut, recognizable shape. Two responses of this kind are:

Card VI (D_2):	A rocket blasting off.
Card VII (D_4):	Flags blowing in the wind.

The mF scoring is used when there is some evidence of form but it has a vague, ambiguous quality. Exemplifying this kind of percept are:

Card VII (W):	Several boulders dangerously balanced on one another, ready to tumble.
Card X (W):	A brilliant display of exploding fireworks of all different kinds.

The last type of inanimate movement score, m, is reserved for percepts where there is a complete absence of form as in the following:

Card V (W):	It reminds me of deterioration—something coming apart.
Card IX (W):	Chaos and turmoil, a head-on clash of the good and evil forces.

COLOR RESPONSES

Chromatic Color Scores: FC, CF, and C

As the name indicates, a response of this type reflects the use of blot colors in the subject's concept. Color percepts may be divided into chromatic and achromatic categories. In the former, such colors as red, green, brown, and orange are integrated into the concept. Achromatic color responses, on the other hand, entail the use of black, gray, and white as colors.

There is a further subdivision of chromatic color responses into natural and arbitrary color percepts. The natural color classification signifies the use of a color ordinarily associated with the percept being described, in its usual state. Essentially, this means that there is no incongruity between the color chosen and the object or creature as it is generally seen. By contrast, the arbitrary use of color indicates a forced quality or what might be termed the use of color in a colorless way—i.e., the particular color chosen for the concept is irrelevant and any other color would be equally appropriate.

There are, in turn, three kinds of natural chromatic color scores. The first, FC, is employed when a color component is combined with a definite and well-recognized shape and, additionally, the color is in consonance with the concept. Samples of this type of percept are:

Card III (D_1):   A very pretty red bow.

Card X (D_{13}):   The green color and the shape suggest grasshoppers.

The same scoring criteria apply to a CF scoring as to FC, with the exception that in the former, the contours are less definite, i.e., the percept is less form controlled. For example:

Card II (D_1):   They resemble blood stains.

Card IX (D_6):   These look very much like scoops of strawberry ice cream.

The third subclassification of natural chromatic color response is reserved for pure color concepts where form is entirely absent and only color is used in the determination of the percept. The symbol C is employed to convey the presence of pure color. An example is:

Card VIII (D_4):   The blue is water.

It would not be justified, however, to score the above type of response C if it occurred only once in the record; if it occurred only once, one should assign it a CF scoring. However, if the subject perseverated the concept water in association to the blue areas on Cards IX and X as well as VIII, and the response in each instance was without visible shape and any kind of relationship to other portions of the blot, then C would be the appropriate scoring.

There are several other variations of C response scoring. The first of these is color naming, using the symbol C_n to reflect that the subject simply enumerated the various hues in the card. Color naming should not be scored loosely and must meet several strict criteria, foremost of which is that the subject must state unequivocally that he or she is making a response rather than offering a comment or a remark about the card. In addition, there must be no other more adequate color responses in subsequent responses to that inkblot. A second variation is called color description, C_{des}; this is used when the subject goes somewhat beyond color naming and endeavors to describe certain qualities of the colors. An example of C_{des} would be labeling the colors "a delicate blending of pastels which merge with one another."

The category of arbitrary color responses essentially is used for colors employed in an artificial or colorless manner, perhaps merely to demarcate various blot areas. An arbitrary use of color occurs most frequently in anatomical and map percepts. When the form is distinct and recognizable, the scoring is F/C. Examples of F/C are:

Card VIII (W):	The organs of the human body: the ribs and the lungs and the intestines. It might be a colored medical chart in an anatomy book.
Card IX (D_6):	Pink frogs even though there are no frogs that color.

The C/F scoring category is reserved for the arbitrary use of color in a percept with less definite shape. Examples of such percepts are:

Card IX (W):	A map with a different color for each country. They don't look like any countries in particular.
Card X (D_9):	Pink clouds, though you never see clouds quite that color.

Achromatic Color Scores: FC′, C′F, and C′

The achromatic scores are the exact counterparts of the chromatic scoring categories but, as mentioned before, are used only when black, gray or white are the colors included in the formation of the concept. Once again, the three subdivisions of this scoring category are on a continuum of distinctness of form. The FC′ responses are scored when form is most definite and easily recognized. Illustrations of FC′ scoring are:

Card V (W):	The whole thing looks like a huge black bat.
Card VII (upper two-thirds):	They look like two little gray poodles.

C′F, the intermediate achromatic scoring subcategory, reflects the presence of some form dimension, but of a secondary and vague or very variable type. The following are C′F responses:

Card VI (center gray and black areas): The contrasting gray and black colors make it look like a forbidding crater somewhere on the moon.

Card VIII (white area immediately above lower pink): Mounds of white snow.

As in the instance of chromatic color, C' is scored for achromatic color without any designation of form whatsoever. Such responses are:

Card IV (W): A black stormy sky.

Card VII (the whole card plus the center white area): The white of day and the black of night.

Color Symbolism: FC_{sym}, CF_{sym}, C_{sym}

The symbolic scoring categories are used when the colors in the subject's concept represent symbols of some sort. Once again, the model of the continuum of structured or definite form to unstructured or indefinite form is employed. The FC_{sym} scoring is appropriate when the color is used symbolically in conjunction with a clearly delineated object. Examples of such responses are:

Card X (D_{10}): A cowardly lion. The yellow signifies cowardice.

Card VIII (D_6, card held sideways): Baby girls in pink outfits, the pink symbolizes that they are girls.

The CF_{sym} percepts are those in which some degree of form, albeit indistinct, is present and, once again, the color is used in a symbolic manner. The following percepts are scored CF_{sym}:

Card X (W): An abstract painting composed of many different colors and shapes intertwining with one another, symbolizing the complexity of life.

Card X (D_5): A peculiarly shaped green object, probably a fertility symbol.

C_{sym} is scored when color is employed to convey an abstract idea, with form totally omitted from the percept. Two examples of color symbolism responses are:

Card II (D_1):   The red part stands for passion.
Card VIII (D_4):   I don't know what this is other than
                                    symbolizing a blue mood.

It should be noted here that the various achromatic scoring categories, namely, FC', C'F, and C', can be appended with a symbolic notation in order to indicate the symbolic use of white, gray, and black in a percept, just as color symbolism is scored. Symbolic achromatic responses, however, tend to be considerably less frequent than the chromatic variety.

SHADING RESPONSES: c, K, and k

Shading responses are scored when the subject uses the nuances of shading of achromatic or chromatic inkblot areas in the formation of the percept. There are essentially three broad classifications of shading scores: surface and texture; three-dimensional or depth scores either as distance or diffusion; and lastly, a three-dimensional conception projected on a two-dimensional plane. The notion of definiteness of form applies to all shading responses just as it does to all color concepts. Again, there is a three-fold subdivision based on whether the form of the percept is definite and distinct, vague or variable, or entirely without shape.

Surface or Texture Responses: Fc, cF, and c

An Fc is scored when the shading aspects of the blot are employed to describe a certain surface impression such as roughness, or a carved effect, and the form is definite. A scoring of Fc is also appropriate when an object has an indefinite shape, but the subject uses shading nuances to indicate a very finely differentiated texture effect, as in a piece of very silky material.
Some examples of Fc scoring are:

Card IV (W):   A bearskin with a thick and furry appearance.
Card VI (D_3):   An artistically carved, highly polished
                                    bedpost.
Card VII (D_1):   Granite-like rock that has been worn smooth
                                    and is very pleasant to the touch.
Card VIII (D_4):   Some pieces of silky-like material with an
                                    interesting design woven into it.

In comparison to Fc, where the form may be quite definite, cF is scored when a shading component is used in a percept having indefinite shape and in which the surface impression itself is not highly differentiated. The following are cF type responses:

Card IV (W):   A piece of meat wrapped up in cellophane.

Card VI (W, top and   Just a piece of fur of some sort.
side extensions cut
off):

A c or pure texture response is a percept where shape is entirely ignored, and shading is used in an essentially undifferentiated manner. Examples of c responses are:

Card VII (W):   All of it looks so soft, just like cotton.

Card I (W):   The whole thing gives a slimy spongy feeling—something you wouldn't want to touch unless you had to.

Distance and Diffusion Scores: FK, KF, and K

The scoring FK is given for all vista percepts when shading is used to describe distance between several objects or between two parts of the same percept. Illustrations of FK scoring are:

Card II (the dark areas   A landscape with woods and hills, a castle in
and the white space):   the distance set near the shore of a lake.

Card III (D3):   A three-dimensional view of the pelvis—you can see the front bones and the back bones.

Contrasted with a definite form implicit in an FK scoring, KF is utilized when the outline of the percept is unclear and the impression is given of space-filling diffusion. Examples are:

Card VII (W):   Clouds of different shapes.

Card IX (D_8):   It looks like water coming out in a very fine spray, almost a mist.

When there is no visible form and the concepts denote space-filling diffusion, the scoring is K. Fog or room-encompassing darkness on any of the cards would qualify for a K scoring.

Three-Dimensional Space Projected on a Two-Dimensional Plane: Fk, kF, and k

This category of shading score is used for x-rays and topographical maps. Once again, the definiteness of the form determines whether Fk, kF, or k is appropriately scored. When the x-ray is of a specific part of the body or the topographical map is of a particular country or region, then Fk is scored in preference to kF. Pure k is rarely scored, as both maps and x-rays have some element of form. If the subject's statement itself is vague, such as "it gives an x-ray-like impression," this would be scored k.

MULTIPLE DETERMINANTS

A subject may utilize more than one determinant in developing a percept. There are many commonplace double determinant combinations and, occasionally, a triple determinant is warranted. When it appears as if more than three determinants are required, however, it is very likely that several responses are actually involved, each of which should be scored separately. Examples of multiple determinant scoring are:

Card II (D$_3$):	Two bears, they look furry, black bears (D Fc·FC').
Card II (W):	Reminds me of two witches dangling. They have their hands and legs up. They're wearing black coats and pointed red hats (W M·FC·FC').
Card III (D$_2$):	Bright red blood dripping down (D CF·mF).
Card III (black areas):	Two cannibals over a big pot. The black makes me say cannibals. The bottom part is the pot with some gray smoke coming from it (D M·FC'·KF).
Card VIII (D$_4$):	A bluish mist with dim forms in it (D CF·KF).
Card X (D$_8$):	Two bluebirds flying toward each other (D FM·FC).

4

Scoring Populars, Form-Level, and the Simple Content Categories

SCORING FOR CONTENT

Content refers to the nature of what is actually seen by the subject in contrast to the perceptual processes involved. Basically, content is concerned with the associations the subject offers to the inkblot material and not with the aspects of the blot (form, movement, color, and shading) that determine what was seen. There is literally no end to the number of possible scoring categories for content. Generally speaking, however, the majority of associations fall within the three major categories of humans, animals, and objects. When a response appears to defy classification into one of the more usual content scoring categories, then a special category may be added. Such special categories may be especially significant in a Rorschach record if the particular content is perseverated. For example, if the subject gives the response "reminds me of death" to a number of the cards, it would be most important and significant to have this reflected in a content scoring category.

Human Content: H, Hd, (H), and (Hd)

There are fundamentally four types of human content scoring. The first type covers content pertaining to the perception of a whole human figure or a major part of it. The symbol designated for this type of human content is H. An example of a concept scored H is:

Card III: Two people carrying something.

A second type of human content scoring possible is human detail, Hd.

This category is reserved for percepts involving a portion of the human figure. Illustrative of this kind of content is:

Card II (upper center,   Two hands pressed together as if in the act of
small usual detail):   prayer.

It should be noted that the Hd scoring is restricted to body parts that are associated with living human beings rather than anatomical concepts.

The third subcategory under human content is (H), indicating that the human figure is removed from reality to some degree, i.e., a piece of sculpture, a caricature, or, conceivably, a mythological figure. A typical (H) response scoring is:

Card IX (orange   Two witches casting a spell.
portions):

There is also (Hd) scoring which conveys that only a portion of a caricature drawing or imaginary human figure is involved in the percept. Exemplifying this kind of response is:

Card X (upper third of   Just the heads of two little elves.
pink areas):

Animal Scoring: A, Ad, (A), and (Ad)

The symbol A is scored for percepts depicting a whole or almost complete animal figure. For example:

Card X (lower green):   Two caterpillars.

Again, consistent with the human detail scoring, Ad is the content category used when only a part of an animal is perceived. A response of this type is:

Card IV (lower center   A bull's head with big horns.
small usual detail):

There is also an (A) scoring for animal-like monsters, mythological animals, and caricatures or sculptures of animal figures. This symbol is also used when the concept of the animal is unrealistic because it is humanized. A good example of (A) scoring is:

Card V: A strange rabbit in some kind of costume.
                           From the way it is standing on its toes, it
                           might be in a ballet.

Parts of animals which are unrealistic representations are scored (Ad), such as:

Card I (side large
details):

Heads of dragons with their mouths wide
open.

Object Scores: Obj, H$_{obj}$, A$_{obj}$

Another type of content category scoring pertains to various types of objects. The symbol Obj is used for a response that involves a man-made object, for example:

Card II (upper red):   A pair of red socks.

There are also human objects, H$_{obj}$, and animal objects, A$_{obj}$, content scoring classifications. The former is used specifically for objects very intimately related to humans. An example is:

Card X (central
portion of inner blue):

A skillfully shaped false tooth which a dentist
is probably getting ready to put into
someone's mouth.

The scoring A$_{obj}$ is appropriate when a part of an animal's body is being used ornamentally, or possibly, practically. The following illustrates A$_{obj}$ content:

Card VI: A fur rug.

Card X (small center
orange area):

A wishbone from a chicken.

Other Content Categories:
At, A$_{at}$, Sex, N, Geo, Pl, Art, and Abs

As noted before, there are almost an unlimited number of possible content categories. Others which occur with reasonable frequency include anatomy, At, which is scored for an anatomical treatment of parts of the human body. An At scoring would be given for:

Card VIII (upper
center dark area and
extensions emanating
from it):

Human spinal column and some ribs
diagrammed in a medical book.

There is also an animal anatomy scoring, A$_{at}$, for sections of an animal seen anatomically, such as in an anatomy chart.

Any percept pertaining to sexual organs or sexual activity receives the scoring Sex. This includes anatomical responses where there is a clear intent to convey some aspect of sexual functioning. Clear-cut examples of Sex content responses are:

| Card VI (upper extension): | A penis. |
| Card VII (lower center darker area): | A vagina. |

Whenever a natural landscape is seen involving such features of nature as rivers, forests, mountains, and, conceivably, a sunset, the scoring is N, nature. However, rivers, lakes, and islands not seen as part of a landscape are scored geography, Geo, as are topographical features explicitly seen as a portion of a map or scientific representation. Plants and flowers receive the scoring Pl.

The symbol Art is utilized for paintings, designs, or various drawings in which no specific content is identified. If a subject, for example, describes Card X as "modern art" the appropriate scoring would be Art. Lastly, the symbol Abs, standing for abstract, denotes a percept where once again there is no specific content, and what is being conveyed is merely an idea. The content category abstract would be used for a percept such as:

| Card II: | Just a feeling of forces of various kinds acting on one another. |

Other content categories that occur with some frequency include X-ray, Oral, Food, Anal, Map, Clouds, Smoke, Geometry, Architecture, Alphabet, Clothing, Botany, Landscape, Water, Aggression, Explosion, Blood, Fire, Ice, Music, Science, Religion, Eyes, and Mask responses. As noted above, however, the content categories mentioned in this chapter are not designed to be all-inclusive, and content scorings may be assigned to responses that do not fall easily into the above categories.

POPULAR AND ORIGINAL RESPONSES

This aspect of content scoring is basically concerned with frequency of occurrence of particular responses to specific blot areas. The symbol P denotes a commonplace percept, that is, one which occurs with a high degree of frequency. Unfortunately, there has been no real agreement on what constitutes a "frequent" response. Some Rorschach workers state that a popular response is a percept found in 1 in 3 records, while others feel that 1 in 10 is sufficiently frequent to warrant the label popular. There are also problems of the same sort with respect to an O or original response, though here there is somewhat more agreement that an original designation should not be used for responses that occur more often than 1 in 100 records. Most responses found in a given record are, of course, neither original nor popular, but rather fall somewhere between the extremes of being very ordinary or highly unique.

It is recommended that the popular scoring be restricted to percepts found in Beck's list of populars, which is reproduced in Table 4-1. We view the Beck populars as preferable to those presented by Klopfer, both because of the more specific statistical criteria he uses in setting up the populars and because of the greater possible range of his scores.

Original percepts are somewhat difficult to score even for the most experienced Rorschach worker and are virtually impossible to identify by a Rorschach student. Responses that seem very different and creative for the neophyte Rorschach scorer may in fact be found in Rorschach protocols with some frequency. Hertz (1970) labels various original responses in her tables,

Table 4-1
Beck's Popular Responses

Card I:	Bat, moth, or butterfly (W).
	Human form (D_3 and D_1) (May be child or woman, either whole or incomplete).
Card II:	Two humans (W).
	Butterfly or moth (D_1).
	Bear or dog (D_3).
Card III:	Two humans or representations of humans. Butterfly, bowtie, ribbon, or variations of these (D_1).
Card IV:	Animal skin, hide, pelt, or rug, or human dressed in animal skin coat, or a massive, furry animal (W).
	Human foot or shoe (D_3). Boot or human leg (D_2).
Card V:	Bat, moth, or butterfly (W).
	Animal or human leg, with muscle element involved (upper half of d_2).
Card VI:	Animal skin, hide, pelt, or rug: (W) or (D_1).
Card VII:	Human heads, faces, women's heads (D_3) or whole human (W).
Card VIII:	Animals (D_1). However, if a specific animal is named, bears, rodents, beavers, muskrats, squirrels, and cats (lions, tigers, etc.), they are considered popular.
Card IX:	Head, face of a human, or a named person such as Winston Churchill (D_4).*
Card X:	Crab, lobster, or spider (D_1).
	Dog or special breed of dog (D_{10}).
	Rabbit's head or variations (bunny's head, etc.—D_7).

Adapted from Beck, S. J., Beck, A. G., Levitt, E. E., and Molish, H. B. *Rorschach's test. I: Basic Processes.* New York: Grune & Stratton, 1961.

*This response is scored as a popular, regardless of the position of the card. If the subject turns Card IX and sees a human head, a popular is scored. All of the other 19 popular forms are scored P only if the card is held in the upright position.

and these tables can be used to provide some basis for scoring originality. It should be pointed out, however, that in our opinion, Hertz is somewhat overly liberal in characterizing a percept as original and, therefore, her tables can serve as no more than a general guide. Original responses can have a minus designation, implying that the percept is bizarre or incongruent with the configuration of a particular inkblot.

FORM LEVEL SCORING

Form level describes how well the percept given by the subject conforms to the inkblot outline. Several systems have been developed for scoring form quality, including one by Klopfer, Ainsworth, Klopfer, and Holt (1954), which endeavor to rate form on a numerical scale. For various reasons, these approaches have proved somewhat unsatisfactory, and assessing form quality with confidence and reliability remains a frustratingly elusive aspect of Rorschach scoring.

The approach described here tries to obviate some of the complexities of dealing with form quality, and, if anything, may err in the direction of being too simplistic. In the present system, form quality is scored in two categories: + for good or average form, and − for poor form. Several components are considered in the judgment of form quality. The first, accuracy, is indicative of the degree of agreement between the configurations of the inkblots and the concepts offered by the subject. Accuracy relates to the definiteness with which the subject describes the percept. For example, a subject can give a precisely outlined response of two people on Card III, identifying the head, torso extremities, and other details of the figures. By contrast, a subject can also elect to limit responses to those having fairly indefinite or varied shapes, such as rocks or flowers. If the subject gives fairly well-delineated percepts to areas of the inkblots that match the percept, then, obviously, adequate form is present. If a distinctly shaped concept is at variance with a section of the blot chosen, then poor form quality is clearly the case.

Single determinant concepts with an indefinite or semidefinite form are the most difficult to score because the inkblots, per se, are not really structured to comply with any single concept. In most cases, therefore, responses that are only quasidefinite, having a somewhat amorphous quality, cannot be readily scored poor form. Sometimes, however, a vaguely defined percept is located in a fairly distinct blot area that is strictly at variance with the concept and, in these instances, a minus form level scoring is indicated. An example of the latter would be:

Card III: The whole thing looks like some kind of fish.

Another consideration in evaluating form level is the degree of elaboration involved in the subject's percept. In some instances, there is virtually no attempt to delineate the response in detail and, in other instances, a great effort is made to point out various parts that make the percept much clearer. Amplifications and elaborations can be redundant, or, in less frequent instances, can bring in details which, in effect, spoil the concept and give it a minus form quality. An example of the last type of elaborating process is the following:

Card V: A bat with its wings spread in flight. It is
                                 shaped just like a bat, but I see these things
                                 coming out of the wings as lizards' mouths.

An organizational component also enters into the assessment of form quality. Some subjects omit certain of the blot areas or bring them into loose relationship with other areas, whereas other subjects can develop much more meaningful interrelationships between various blot parts. As in the case of elaboration discussed above, organizational efforts can be seriously flawed and largely undermine a response that initially had good form. An example of this:

Card X: An underwater scene with various kinds of
                                 fish swimming around. The pink in the center
                                 are big pieces of coral which the blue fish in
                                 the middle are towing in the water.

Rather than relying strictly on one's own judgment to determine the consonance between the concept and the inkblot with respect to form, it is suggested that Hertz's frequency tables be used as a reference supplemented by the form quality tables found in Exner's text (1974). A very large number of percepts and their locations are included in these two sets of tables, and each response is designated as good or poor form.

With respect to the Hertz tables, it is our experience that some of the minus scorings are, in fact, rather average form quality and, therefore, should be properly classed as plus responses. Thus, her minus form level scorings should be treated somewhat circumspectly. On the other hand, one can have confidence that any percept she scores as having good form has indeed complied with the criteria for adequate form level, and should always receive a plus scoring.

5

Tabulation and Quantitative Interpretation

TABULATION OF SCORES AND COMPUTATION OF PERCENTAGES AND RATIOS

The tabulation process and the subsequent computation of percentages and ratios are essentially an effort to summarize the subject's Rorschach performance, and to analyze it from a number of standpoints. While there are some commercial forms available to facilitate this process, the student can do just as well by utilizing some blank sheets of paper and carefully following the procedures outlined below.

The initial step in tabulation is to collect the Rorschach responses from all 10 cards and make up a scoring summary sheet (see sample summary sheets in Chapter 12). The summary sheet consists of listing the reaction time and total time for each of the 10 cards, plus the scoring for every response. In addition to noting the location, determinant, and content scoring and denoting, where appropriate, whether the percept is a plus or minus form level and a popular or original, a one or several word description of the response should be included. Rather than thumbing through numerous Rorschach responses forms, the clinician then works entirely with the single summary sheet which gives an overview of the test performance, the sequence of responses, and, most importantly, reduces the possibility of errors in tabulating. One note of caution might be sounded here: Clinicians who score the Rorschach during the inquiry are well advised, before proceeding with the summary sheet, to review the responses in more reflective and leisurely fashion to make certain that the scoring is indeed correct.

Once the clinician is confident of the scoring, the percepts are tallied in the various categories on a sheet as shown in Table 5-1.

Several features of this tabulation sheet might be pointed out. First, any location, determinant, or content subclassification which does not occur in a particular record need not be listed on the tabulation sheet: e.g., if Fc were missing from a protocol, then it would be omitted from the tabulation sheet.

Second, multiple determinants and multiple content are treated as a unit when listing and, in the case of determinants, when figuring F + %. For other tabulations, however, each part is considered separately.

Minus scores are added to the plus scores for the same symbol with a bracketed number next to the total to indicate the number that were minus. Additional responses, i.e., those appearing during the inquiry, are represented

Table 5-1
Rorschach Test: Tabulation Sheet

Location	Determinants		Content	
W	F	FC'	H	Aggression
W(S)			(H)	Alphabet
W̶	M	C'F	Hd	Anal
	FM	C'	(Hd)	Architecture
D				Blood
D(S)	Fm	FC	A	Botany
	mF	F/C	(A)	Clothing
d	m		Ad	Clouds
d(S)		CF	(Ad)	Explosion
	Fk	C/F		Eyes
dd	kF		Obj	Fire
de	k	C_{des}	H_{Obj}	Food
di		C_{sym}	A_{Obj}	Ice
Dd { dr	FK	C		Landscape
(S) with any	KF	C_n	At	Map
of above	K		A_{at}	Masks
		Multiple		Music
	Fc	Determinants	Sex	Oral
S	cF		N	Religion
S(D)	c		Geo	Science
S(d)			Pl	Smoke
S (with any			Art	Water
Dd category			Abs	X-ray
responses)				
DW				Multiple Content
				(*continued*)

Table 5-1 (continued)

Number of responses (R)_____　　Consider additionals separately

Rejections:　Cards_____
Number of P_____　　　　　　　Not more than 20 possible—
Number of O_____　　　　　　　　Beck's List

Average R/T chromatic:　　　　　　　　Sum of reaction times to Cards
　　　　　　　　　　　　　　　　　　　　II, III, VIII, IX, X ÷ 5

Average R/T achromatic:　　　　　　　　Sum of reaction times to Cards I,
　　　　　　　　　　　　　　　　　　　　IV, V, VI, VII ÷5

F%_____　　　　　　　　　　Number of pure F ÷ by R × 100
F+%_____

Treat multiple determinant as a unit. Consider only form dominant responses (M, FM, Fm, Fk, FK, F, Fc, FC', F/C and FC) in the calculation of F+%. If a part of a multiple determinant is not form dominant, then the multiple determinant response is omitted entirely from the F+% computation. Multiple determinants which are partially poor form are treated as if the whole percept is —. Total number of + single and + multiple determinant responses in which form is dominant should be divided by the sum of + and − form dominant responses × 100.

A%_____　　　　　　　　　　Sum of A, (A), Ad, and (Ad) ÷ R
　　　　　　　　　　　　　　　　　　　× 100

H%_____　　　　　　　　　　Sum of H, (H), Hd, and (Hd) ÷ R ×
　　　　　　　　　　　　　　　　　　　100

Any other content percent that seems　　10% or more
significant

W:M_____　　　　　　　　　　W includes W(S), WX, and WX(S) but
　　　　　　　　　　　　　　　　　　　omits DW

Sum C_____　　　　　　　　　Sum of color responses weighted
　　　　　　　　　　　　　　　　　　　as follows:
　　　　　　　　　　　　　　　　　　　1/2—FC　　1—CF　　1 1/2—C
　　　　　　　　　　　　　　　　　　　　　　　　　　　　　　　C_{des}
　　　　　　　　　　　　　　　　　　　　　　F/C　　　C/F　　C_{sym}
　　　　　　　　　　　　　　　　　　　　　　　　　　　　　　　C_n

M: sum C_____

m:c_____ m includes FM, Fm, mF, and m
c includes Fc, cF, c, FC', C'F, C'

VIII–X%_____ Total number of responses to Cards
VIII, IX, and X ÷ R × 100

FK + F + Fc%_____ Sum of FK, F, and Fc ÷ R × 100.
Should be equal to or larger than
F%

(H + A):(Hd + Ad)_____ Includes H, (H), A, (A), Hd, (Hd), Ad,
and (Ad) but not H_{obj} or A_{obj}

Apperception: W____% D____% d____% Dd and S (pure S)____%

Determine Use of Areas from Following Table

W		D		d		Dd and S	
((W))	10%	((D))	30%				
(W)	11–20	(D)	31–45	(d)	5%		
W	21–30	D	46–55	d	6–15	Dd S	10%
W̲	31–45	D̲	56–65	d̲	16–25	Dd S̲	11–15
W̳	46–60	D̳	66–80	d̳	26–35	Dd S̳	16–20
W̳	≥ 61	D̳	≥ 81	d̳	≥36	Dd S̳	≥ 21

Intellectual Level____ (Determine Approximate Level from Following Table)

Level	Very Superior 130	High Average to Superior 110	Average 100	Dull Normal 90	Inferior Retarded 70
F+%	90–100	80–89	70–79	60–69	60
M	5	4–5	2–3	1	0 or poor Ms
W	7	4–7	2–3	1	0 or poor Ws
A%	30	30–39	40–49	50–69	70–100

by plus signs and listed next to the appropriate symbol in brackets, but do not count in the total. Some examples of minus and additional scoring notations are:

1. Six responses scored FM, of which three were minus and two were additional, would be listed FM = 4 (−3) (+2).
2. Three responses scored Fc, all of which were minus, would be noted as Fc = 3 (−3).
3. Four responses scored CF, all additional, would be tabulated as CF = (+4).
4. Five responses scored M, no minuses, no additionals, would be entered as simple M = 5.

After the tabulations are completed, percentages and ratios are computed as indicated above.

QUANTITATIVE INTERPRETATION

Analysis of percentages and ratios of the sundry Rorschach scoring categories can be exceedingly useful. One should be well aware, however, that the empirical evidence for the validity of the meaning of various location and determinant categories and percentages and ratios utilizing these components of the Rorschach is short of compelling. On the other hand, there are a great deal of less formal clinical data in consensual agreement with regard to what various quantitative aspects of the record mean. The most judicious posture that a Rorschach worker can assume in dealing with quantitative material, therefore, is to treat these interpretations as working hypotheses subject to corroboration or rejection based on other sources of information about the test subject. These other data pertaining to the individual being evaluated might include qualitative aspects of the Rorschach, test behavior, performance on other tests in the battery, and anamnestic data regarding such variables as age, sex, socioeconomic background, and other relevant historical factors.

The Rorschach worker should never attach an inordinate degree of significance to a single percentage or ratio, but rather should look for interrelationships between variables and endeavor to determine whether a meaningful configuration exists. Furthermore, while 1 of the 10 cards may have traumatic impact for a subject, the subject's performance on all 10 must be carefully considered, with the sequencing of responses within each card and for the set of cards, per se, receiving special attention. Only by searching for patterns of personality factors by scrutinizing a variety of test results and behavioral and background features can the clinician arrive at a genuinely revealing picture.

There is material on the tabulation sheet that does not enter directly into the calculation of various percentages and ratios. This includes the additional responses. In making interpretations, the Rorschach worker should carefully review additionals, for they may either confirm or dilute certain interpretations that were made on the basis of the more formal record. A protocol composed of a relatively small number of primarily stereotyped responses would be interpreted quite differently if the subject also had given a number of fairly imaginative additional responses in the inquiry phase of testing. One must also carefully examine the quality of various location and determinant scorings as well as consider the percentages and ratios. Two subjects may have the same W% but a very different interpretation would be in order if one of them adhered to vague, poorly defined W's and the other gave whole responses that were very well integrated and highly creative. Both animal and human movement in particular lend themselves to much latitude in quality.

What are presented in the following pages of this chapter are interpretive guidelines of a very general and comparatively elementary type. For a more in-depth consideration of the interpretation of quantitative aspects of the Rorschach, the worker should consult more advanced texts. Among those which can be especially recommended as compatible with the approach of this book are Klopfer et al. (1954), Schachtel (1966), and, specifically for diagnostic assistance, Schafer (1948). As stated before, when assigning interpretative meanings to various Rorschach location determinant content areas, one is dealing with material that is essentially hypothetical and, therefore, requires corroboration from as many other sources as possible.

Location Scores

The location areas basically reflect the intellectual approach the subject uses in dealing with various situations. The average range of scores for the different types of location areas are W, 20–30%; D, 45–50%; d, 5–15%; and Dd and S, < 10% (see Chapter 6 for more detailed normative data). The use of percentages adjusts for the total number of responses given by a subject.

While each of the location, determinant, and content scorings will be treated separately, it cannot be overemphasized that Rorschach ratios and percentages should be treated configurationally, and that one particular aspect of the scoring profile should not be considered in isolation, un-influenced by other elements of the subject's performance.

In general, W responses are thought to relate to organizational ability. Before making any assumptions about W's, however, it is necessary to assess their quality; that is, are they good or poor form. The whole responses that reflect good form might suggest strong conceptualization and a capacity to deal with the abstract. On the other hand, W's of a very mundane or even poor quality could possibly derive from the intellectual operations of an individual who has high aspirations for him- or herself without the ability to achieve them. It may be posited that a low W percentage may be consistent with minimal organizational drive and disinterest in seeking interrelation-ships between diverse aspects of experience. As will be discussed under movement, the number of W's should also be examined within the framework of the number of M's the subject produces.

The presence of cutoff W's may indicate critical proclivities which can have constructive components or be compulsively disruptive. Responses that warrant a DW scoring may reveal inadequate reality testing in the form of a tendency to indulge in very unreflective overgeneralization.

The D and d percentages, when they occur in the average range, can best be interpreted as appropriate, commonsense, and practical application of intelligence probably resulting in a successful coping style with the environmental demands of everyday living. When there is an exaggerated number of the two types of usual details, it may be hypothesized that the subject feels somewhat anxious, insecure, and possibly inadequate and, as a consequence, limits Rorschach responses to the mundane and stereotyped, avoiding anything that is not obvious. More than 15 percent of d is sometimes found in a carping, highly pedantical individual. A low percentage of D's usually results in an inordinate number of W's, which then have to be examined for quality and interpreted in keeping with the suggestions made above.

The scoring category of Dd and S may not be present in a particular record, and no special significance should be attached to its absence. When Dd's do occur, many interpretations are possible, ranging from an imaginative responsiveness to one's surroundings, to a hyperalert, obsessive interaction with the environment. More specifically, the Dd percept is most germane for interpreting compulsive or obsessive thinking. A number of de responses may be compatible with an anxious individual who resists engaging the environment and maintains the majority of relationships on a superficial, noninvolving level.

Responses scored di are also reflective of anxiety and some concern with social relationships. The dr percept may be most reflective of a great deal of sensitivity and perceptiveness, but may also occur with autistic thinking. An inordinate number of S concepts are found in personalities with strong negativistic and oppositional tendencies. When space responses are coupled with good whole responses, they may indicate inner strength and an appropriate capacity to assert oneself.

Determinant Scorings

Forms Scores

The percentages of pure form responses normally ranges from 30 to 50 percent. If the percentage is greater than 50, considerable rigidity and constriction may be present. In essence, the higher the F%, the more conventional and unspontaneous the subject. By contrast, an F% less than 30 is found in compulsive individuals who readily personalize situations. The production of large numbers of pure F's requires the least degree of energy and investment on the part of the subject. Thus, a record abounding in F's may be consistent with a defensively evasive individual. On the other hand, a person with very limited emotional and intellectual resources may also produce such a record. It is especially necessary to interpret the F% in light of the presence of other form-dominant responses such as M, FC, and Fc which, when occurring in any numbers, may reveal substantial personality assets, counterbalancing either a high or low number of F's.

Movement Scores

Movement (including human movement, animal movement, and inanimate movement) generally relates to an individual's ideational activity, empathy, maturity, capacity for delayed gratification, and living with oneself.

M, or human movement, is probably the most critical of all determinants to be found in a Rorschach protocol. It must be remembered that the M response entails a projective process, namely, ascribing movement to an inkblot. It also involves the very complex and demanding task of describing human attributes. Thus, M clearly relates to imagination and elements of identification and empathy with other people. An average number of M's in a record would be around three, with a person offering this number likely to be reasonably intelligent, well-integrated, and fairly creative, with potential for maintaining successful social relationships.

In contrast to M, FM (animal movement) reflects the less mature aspects of personality which are not under the same degree of conscious control and may be manifested in difficulties in controlling immediate gratification of impulse life. At the same time, some FM should be present as such responses represent a source of energy and vitality and are, in fact, a precursor of M percepts. This latter is especially true in young children where a record with a number of FM responses would be regarded positively and, with the maturing process, it would be conjectured that many of the FM's would be translated into M types of movement.

The inanimate-type movement percept (encompassing Fm, mF, and m) is generally associated with unpleasant feelings indicative of repressed conflicts and tension. Two or more m responses may indicate that the individual is experiencing marked stress and sees his or her situation as growing progressively more out of control. In that m indicates that the individual is aware of threatening feelings, an absence of m type responses, when the individual is in an obvious conflict situation, has very negative implications. In a normal record, the proportion of the various types of movement responses should be about two M's, one FM, and one-half m.

The W to M ratio is very important in the quantitative interpretation. The ratio of two W's to one M is considered optimal and the interpretation that is suggested is that aspiration level and ability are commensurate. When the W to M ratio exceeds four to one, then it is hypothesized that aspiration has moved beyond available resources and is too high. On the other hand, when the W's are less than twice the number of human movement responses, then it is ordinarily posited that the individual is narcissistically preoccupied with his or her daydreams and fantasies, and has not found suitable channels for his or her creative potentials. Movement is also intricately bound up with various types of color responses.

Color Scores

The assumption that is made about color responses (both chromatic and achromatic) is that they reveal much of how the subject deals with and responds to environmental stimuli which, in turn, taps the nature of inter-actions with other people. Color responses may be regarded as located on a continuum, with C on one end of the scale indicative of wild emotionality and impulsivity, and FC, at the other end, consistent with responsiveness and consideration for others. The FC color response may be best described as exemplifying emotional control, i.e., the capacity to react to affectively-charged situations in a socially appropriate manner as would a well-adjusted person. When the FC has an arbitrary component such as in the F/C scoring, it is posited that this outer show of responsiveness is superficial and forced, and that genuine feelings are not really involved.

The CF response, which is intermediate between FC and C, reflects some measure of control but lacks the integration of the FC percept. On the one hand, CF types of responses reflect a degree of uninhibitedness and spontaneity, but when too numerous, some lapse in control. The C/F response, as was the case in F/C, represents a studied attempt to be spontaneously responsive.

The pure C percept, which is entirely without form, suggests an affective explosiveness in which the individual is at the mercy of his or her emotions and cannot exercise any control over them. Color naming (C_n), color descriptions (C_{des}), and color symbolism (C_{sym}) all, in varying degrees, represent some effort to impose restraints over raw feelings, generally with rather poor success. The record of a reasonably well-adjusted person should contain two or three times as many FC's and CF's and no pure C responses.

The M to sum C ratio is highly significant and pivotal in assessing the individual's personality. Essentially, this ratio focuses on the balance between the subject's inner-life and his or her capacity to deal with external stimulation. It may be viewed simplistically as tapping an introversion-extroversion dimension. Generally speaking, it is hypothesized that there should be two or three times as many M's as sum C and that the sum of M and sum C should be at least three. If the record contains too little M, then one may very well be dealing with the selfcentered, infantile personality. By the same token, if there is too much M, then the individual may be overly withdrawn and too immersed in fantasy living. When the sum of M and sum of C is less than three, the subject very likely is constricted in his or her life and reacts in a very inhibited, rigid, colorless, and repressed fashion. When the sum of M and sum C is greater than seven, a very rich and versatile life may be suggested.

The M to sum C ratio should always be contrasted with the m to c ratio, the latter being the more basic tendencies of the individual which are not fully accepted. When these two ratios are in the same direction, this underlines the M to sum C interpretation. When these ratios are at variance with one another, some conflict may exist between behavioral patterns and inner needs.

The percentage of responses to the last three cards is also interpreted as revealing some aspects of the individual's affective life. The expectation is that 30–40 percent of the responses in a particular Rorschach record will be given to these three color cards. The degree of affective responsiveness to these cards in terms of number of responses is conjectured to be less under the individual's conscious control than the manner in which color as such is used in various percepts.

Achromatic color percepts are seen as dilute or toned-down chromatic percepts and merely an extension of the subject's responsiveness to color. When C' type responses of a grey or black variety dominate a protocol, however, it may be surmised that some depressive features are present. C' responses that involve white space may indicate negativism and aggressiveness. In both instances, there is evidence of withdrawal and some unresponsiveness to the environment.

Shading Scores

All shading responses may be interpreted as having an anxiety component within the context of affectional needs and modes of gratifying them. When Fc is the type of texture response that predominates in a record, then it may be hypothesized that one is dealing primarily with an unaggressive, ingratiatingly passive person who is sensitively aware of the feelings of others. While this person may have almost infantile cravings for closeness to others, social interactions are likely to be controlled and quite tactful. In contrast to Fc, cF and c probably represent varying degrees of far more primitive, undifferentiated dependency needs. These affectional yearnings may very well be on an essentially physical contact level. The pure c response in particular may occur in individuals who are markedly infantile in their emotional demands.

The FK kind of response, in contrast to the surface, tactual types of c responses, implies distance and perspective. An FK percept is hypothesized to mean dealing with one's anxiety by engaging in introspection in an effort to understand the nature of the anxiety rather than merely seeking outside sources of support. Thus, FK may be interpreted as reflective of insight and a positive sign of adjustment. The KF and K types of percept are also three-dimensional, but lack form and are far more disruptive in nature than FK. They may be regarded as indicating that the individual has not been able to develop adequate defenses for dealing with anxiety which, consequently, is of a free-floating kind. The Fk, kF, and k percepts which translate three-dimensional space into two dimensions such as X-rays, imply that the subject is attempting to use intellectualization in handling anxiety. The Fk type of response is consistent with at least some measure of intellectual control, whereas kF and k reveal that intellectualization is not working very success-fully in containing anxiety.

As noted earlier, the m to c ratio is used in conjunction with M to C to determine if the person's behavioral patterns are consistent with his or her basic personality.

The FK + F + Fc% is referred to as the extended F% and is basically a measure of refined control. It is hypothesized that the percentage reflects the way tact and insight modify the individual's basic rigidity. Optimally, FK + Fc should be 25–75 percent of pure F. When it is less than 25 percent, long-standing repressive types of defenses may be disrupting the expression of affectional needs. If FK + Fc is more than 75 percent, the individual may be driven by cravings for affection and may operate in a hypersensitive and mostly dependent manner in his or her transactions with others.

Content Scores

Content scores, per se, are manifestations of the diversity and range of the subject's interest. A broad range of associations to the blot material is usually suggestive of good intelligence, whereas a very limited number of content categories may be indicative of limited intellectual ability and reveal something of the subject's defensive operations.

Animal content should be around 55 percent at most and preferably might be no more than 20 percent. A high percentage of human responses is consistent with an interest in other people. Of greater significance than percentages of human and animal percepts is how people or animals are described in the percept; i.e., the nature of their activity and outstanding characteristics.

Both Hd and Ad may indicate anxiety and a wary cautiousness. There normally should be twice the number of H and A responses as Hd and Ad responses. If H + A is less than 50 percent Hd + Ad, the subject may be experiencing considerable anxiety.

Anatomy percepts are generally interpreted as excessive interest in parts of the body which may be of a hypochondriacal kind. Anatomy responses are also interpreted as reflective of intellectual types of defenses.

Among the other content categories which might be mentioned are sexual percepts indicative of sexual or erotic preoccupations, and blood, which may relate to aggressiveness and hostility either expressed inwardly or outwardly. A number of object responses would be consistent with abstract ability and/or a disinterest in people. Eye concepts of various sorts are particularly significant when they occur, and may suggest that the subject feels under critical surveillance and is quite self-conscious. An almost paranoid stance toward the environment may sometimes be indicated.

Content will be discussed much more exhaustively in the latter sections of this text, but it should be pointed out here that a fixed interpretation for specific associations to the cards can be grossly incorrect. It behooves the examiner to look at the Rorschach record in a more comprehensive and penetrating fashion to discern meaningful personality patterns for the specific individual being evaluated.

Populars and Originals

It would be expected that the average record would have seven or so populars or near populars, indicating a capacity to think in a conventional, conforming fashion. Too many populars might be interpreted as overly stereotyped thinking, possibly due to a limited intellect; the subject may also be very anxiety-ridden and cling to the most obvious. Originals of good quality can be compatible with high-level intellectual ability and capacity for creative thinking. On the other hand, originals of minus form level might point to defective reality appreciation.

Form Level

The F+% deals with how well the individual's reality controls are functioning within the framework of accuracy of perception, or the goodness of fit between the inkblot and the response. When there are a number of responses in which the percept is at variance with the configuration of the blot resulting in $-$'s, then the F+% is lowered, suggesting defective reality appreciation. The F+% should normally be in the 80–90 percent range. When it is 70–80 percent, it may be hypothesized that the reality sense is weakened and the person is adjusting on the borderline level. Below 70 percent would be compatible with markedly vitiated logical controls or possibly someone of seriously impaired intelligence. When the F+% rises above 90 and gets into the 95–100 range, then one is likely to be dealing with a rigid, highly perfectionistic person.

Miscellaneous Aspects of the Scoring Profile

The examination of the total number of percepts given to Rorschach cards may reveal a good deal about the person's intellectual abilities. The average adult would give anywhere from 20–40 responses. A record with below 20 responses suggests a constricted personality or a person who has limited cognitive abilities at his or her disposal. A large number of responses may be obtained from a very imaginative subject. However, if the responses are composed largely of small detail-type percepts, this may indicate compulsivity. A reaction time to chromatic cards that is far more rapid than that to achromatic cards may be present in the record of an individual who is highly stimulated by his or her emotions. When the reaction time to the black and white cards is more rapid, the person may be emotionally blocked and defending against the expression of his or her feelings.

Sequence Analysis

The Rorschach worker must examine the summary sheet carefully, looking chronologically at the reaction times and the number and kind of percepts given to each of the 10 cards taken in sequence. A sudden shift to notably poorer form quality, or a reduction in the number of responses may suggest that the particular card is stimulating some very negative associations, undermining the individual's reality testing and productivity. Knowing which types of concepts occur frequently on a particular card is very helpful in carrying out sequence analysis. If a subject gave fairly popular responses through seven of the cards and, then on Card VIII, became quite idiosyncratic in his or her associations, it might be conjectured that the card had special emotional impact. Additional responses are important in the process of sequence analysis and often give very valuable clues as to the nature of the individual's controls and his or her desire to inhibit or censor certain associational material.

The related topic of content sequence analysis will be discussed in Chapter 10.

6

Normative Data

Normative data relevant to the Rorschach test are often sparse, dated, and understandable only in reference to a particular school of scoring. Nonetheless, the examiner who wishes to use the test in a nomothetic manner will require a normative basis for his or her inferences. The following sources of data may, therefore, prove useful in this connection since they are understandable in terms of a Klopfer-based system.

The most comprehensive set of norms for children was presented by Ames, Métraux, Rodell, and Walker (1974). These authors worked with Rorschach records of 650 children, aged 2–10 years, of "mostly highly educated parents" (Ames, et al., 1974, p. xiii). These records were supplemented by the addition of 900 protocols of various levels of socioeconomic status. Levitt and Truumaa (1972) surveyed 162 sources that provided normative data on the Rorschach records of children and adolescents. Using strict criteria for the inclusion of data, these authors reduced the studies to 15 investigations, including the normative studies of the Ames group. Although Levitt and Truumaa distinguished between the records of subjects of average and above-average intelligence, they did not take into account the variables of race and socioeconomic status.

Comprehensive norms for adolescents were also provided by Ames, Métraux, and Walker (1971) in a study of 700 children aged 10–16. The Levitt and Truumaa volume (1972) likewise deals with normative data on adolescents. Comprehensive norms for elderly individuals were prepared by Ames, Métraux, Rodell, and Walker (1973) using 200 subjects over age 70. Ames et al. (1974) also reported expectancies for adult subjects.

LOCATION SCORES

W%

Ames et al. (1974) report that W% remains fairly steady from age 2 through age 10, hovering around 50. However, their findings also indicate that W% increases with decreasing socioeconomic status. The inner city sample consisting primarily of black children obtained W%s in the 70s.

In the summarized Levitt and Truumaa data, W% for subjects of average intelligence dropped gradually from 51 at age 5, to approximately 22 at age 16. Among the bright subjects, a drop was also seen, from approximately 53 percent at age 5, to approximately 44 percent at age 16. According to Ames et al. (1974), there is a general expectancy of between 20 and 30 percent of W's for normal adults.

Among elderly subjects, Ames et al. (1973) determined W% as being 36 among normal elderly subjects, 43 among presenile elderly, and 46 among senile elderly subjects. Thus, a gradual increase in W% is reported as the subject moves toward senescence.

D%

Ames et al. (1974) indicate that D%, for their sample of 2–10-year-olds, ranged from 33 to 48, with an average close to 40. Increased use of D% was seen after 6 years, with a peak at 9 years. Levitt and Truumaa note a gradual decline of D% from 47 at age 5, to approximately 41 percent at age 16 for their bright subjects. Ames et al. (1971) found that the mean D% for their adolescent subjects ranged from a low of 41 at 10 years to a high of 47 at 14 years.

Ames et al. (1974) report an expectancy of between 50 and 70 percent of D's among adults. In their study of elderly subjects, Ames et al. (1973) noted D% of 47, 47, and 45 percent for their normal, presenile, and senile subjects, respectively.

Dd%

In the Ames (1974) study, Dd% is perceived to increase gradually from age 2 to age 6, at which latter point it reaches 15 percent. It is then reported to drop back to 8 percent at age 10. Much smaller Dd%s are indicated by Ames et al. in their inner city sample, ranging from 4 percent at age 5 to a maximum of 8 percent at age 6.

For their adolescent subjects aged 10–16 years, Ames et al. (1971)

found the mean Dd% to be 8 percent. Ames et al. (1974) note the expected occurrence of Dd to be approximately 10 percent for adult subjects. With respect to elderly subjects, Ames et al. (1973) report mean Dd%s of 15, 9, and 8 percent for normal, presenile, and senile elderly subjects, respectively.

DETERMINANTS

Form

For child subjects, Ames et al. (1974) indicate mean F% above 50 for all ages in their sample. The F% determinant is reported to be at its highest at age 2 years (90 percent), declining steadily to a low point of 52 percent at age 7. It is then reported to rise to a mean of 63 percent at 10 years. It should be noted that, in general, Ames et al. (1974) have also found that F% was higher among their inner city subjects than among their other subjects, ranging between 76 percent at age 9, to 91 percent at age 5½. Among adolescent subjects, Ames et al. (1971) report mean F% falling very close to 62 percent at every age except 16 years, when it drops to 56 percent.

Ames et al. (1974) indicate an expectancy for F% of 50 or less in adult records. Among elderly subjects, Ames et al. (1973) indicate F%s of 65, 56, and 57 percent for their subjects aged 70, 80, and 90, respectively.

Human Movement (M)

According to Ames et al. (1974), the average number of M responses increase with age in an almost steady progression from 2 to 10 years. M is reported as being an average of only 0.1 responses at age 2, reaching a maximum of 1.7 responses at age 10. M responses among the inner city sample are considerably fewer, reaching a maximum mean of only 0.7 by age 10.

In their summarized data, Levitt and Truumaa note a steady increase in M responses from a mean of 0.45 at age 5 for their average subjects, to a mean of 2.36 at age 16. For their bright subjects, an average of 1.2 M responses is seen at age 5, gradually increasing to 2.77 by age 16.

Ames et al. (1974) have indicated a general expectancy of two or three M responses in the average adult record. Ames et al. (1973) also observe that a person with superior intelligence might be expected to give five or more M responses in a record. Among their normal, presenile, and senile elderly subjects, Ames et al. (1973) have found mean M responses of 3.3, 1.6, and 0.2, respectively.

Animal Movement (FM)

Ames et al. (1974) report a progression of 0.1 FM responses at 2 years to 1.9 FM responses at 7 years. In general, FM responses increase with age. Like the M-response pattern, FM responses among inner city subjects are found to be fewer. Mean FM responses among inner city subjects were reported by these investigators to range up to only 1.0 at age 9.

Levitt and Truumaa indicate that FM responses for their average and bright groups combined increased from 1.59 at age 5 to a maximum of 2.81 by age 12, decreased slightly thereafter, and reached an average of 2.41 by age 16. Among their adolescent subjects, Ames et al. (1971) indicate a range of 2.0 to 2.5 FM responses for their adolescent subjects, with the exception of age 15 at which a mean of 1.6 is recorded.

Among adult subjects, Ames et al. (1974) note an expectancy of one to two FM responses in a record. Among their elderly subjects, Ames et al. (1973) indicate mean FM responses 2.7, 2.0, and 0.3 in the normal, presenile, and senile elderly subjects, respectively.

Inanimate Movement (m)

Ames et al. (1974) found that m responses do not exceed 0.2 throughout the preschool period, but are seen as increasing after age 5 up to a peak of 0.8 at age 7, thereafter dropping back to about 0.5. Among their inner city subjects, m responses occurred even less frequently, ranging from none at age 5 up to only a maximum average of 0.2 at various ages thereafter.

In the Levitt and Truumaa summary data, an increase in m responses with age is seen in both the average and the bright groups. For the average subjects, mean m responses increased from 0.26 at age 5 to 0.62 by age 16. In the bright subjects, mean m responses increased from 0.44 at age 5 to 0.89 by age 16. Ames et al. (1971) likewise report an increase in m responses as one enters the teenage years.

Ames et al. (1973) reported a decrease in m responses with increasing age among their elderly subjects. At 70 years, a mean m of 0.33 was found, decreasing to 0.28 among their 80-year-old subjects, and to 0.15 among their 90-year-old subjects.

It should be noted that the m responses referred to above include the Fm, mF, and m categories taken together.

Color Responses

Ames et al. (1974) reported a gradual increase in CF responses among children, from near zero at 2 years, to an average of 0.5 approximately from 2½ to 4 years, and to about 1.3 from age 4½ through 7 years. A slow decrease is reported thereafter. Pure C responses show less of a change with development, but do slowly increase to a peak at 7 years. Ames et al. described FC responses as never frequent in childhood, but showing an increasing trend, from virtual absence at 2 years to highs of 0.7 at ages 7 and 9. The inner city sample of Ames shows clearly less responsiveness to color in all three categories (FC, CF, and C).

The Levitt and Truumaa combined data indicate a gradual decrease for C responses, from an average of 0.37 at age 5, to 0.03 responses by age 16. For the CF category, the trend is also a decreasing one, from an average of 1.16 at age 5, to an average of 0.62 by age 13. Between ages 13 and 16, there is a slight increase in the mean number of CF responses (reaching 0.76 by age 16). In the data on adolescents presented by Ames et al. (1971), mean FC responses show little change with age—averaging 0.3 at age 10 and 0.5 by age 16. Little change in mean CF responses is likewise reported by Ames et al., until age 16, at which time a sudden spurt in this type of response is seen (a mean of 1.2 of such responses at age 16). C responses show no particular trend with age in the Ames data on adolescents. The mean number of C responses is 0.2 at age 10 and 0.1 at age 16.

The expectancy of color responses for adult subjects, as noted by Ames et al. (1974), is about 3.0 FC responses, and perhaps one CF response per record. Among the elderly subjects in the Ames et al. study (1973), mean FC responses of 0.38, 0.37, and 0.54 were found for the 70-year-old subjects, the 80-year-old subjects, and the 90-year-old subjects, respectively. Mean CF responses of 0.69, 0.52, and 0.54 were found for the same three groups, respectively.

CONTENT

Human Responses

Ames et al. (1974) report a slow but steady increase in H% from age 2 (average = 3) to age 10 (average = 16). However, this age trend appears to be very much a function of the high socioeconomic status of these children. The age trends in H% were more obscure in children from working-class backgrounds, and they were actually reversed among inner city children, dropping from 22 percent at age 5 to 5 percent at age 8, and increasing again to 12 percent by age 10. One might question whether a white examiner testing a black child may have been a determining factor in the inner city age trend. In the summarized Levitt and Truumaa data, no age trends in H% were found in children of average intelligence. (H% of 11.2 would be expected at all the ages.) In children of above-average intelligence, H% was noted to increase with age, from 10.3 percent at age 5 to 18 percent at age 10.

Ames et al. (1971) reported a relative stabilization of H% for adolescent boys and girls combined. When the sexes were considered separately, they found that the boys dropped from a high of 19.5 percent at age 10 to 13.9 percent at age 15 (16.1 percent at age 16). On the other hand, girls passed from 18.2 percent at age 10 to 21.9 percent at age 15 (20.1 percent at age 16).

Levitt and Truumaa found no relation between age and H% among adolescents of average intelligence; 11.2 percent was expected. They did find that the increase in H% leveled off with age among adolescents of above-average intelligence; it leveled off at about 20 percent in the teenage years.

In summarizing normative data on adults, Ames et al. (1974) state that the general expectancy is of 10–15 percent for H%. Levitt and Truumaa also report an expectancy of 10–20 percent in adults, the more intelligent subjects being in the upper part of the range.

Among elderly subjects, Ames et al. (1973) measured H% at 24, 17, and 5 percent in normal, presenile, and senile subjects, respectively. H% also increased with age among the elderly, from 16 at age 70, to 18 at age 80, and 24 at age 90. This increase with age was also found in the longitudinal data.

Animal Responses (A)

Ames et al. (1974) found that A% described a fairly steady pattern from age 2 through 10. It varied irregularly from a low of 41 percent to a high of 56. A% was also found to vary with socioeconomic status, being higher in the lower social classes. (Among inner city children, average A% was as high as 71 percent at age 8.) Levitt and Truumaa reported little relationship between age and A% among children of either average or above-average intelligence (A% was nearly 50 in these children). Interestingly, these authors did not find that A% varied with intelligence.

Ames et al. (1971) report that A% remained relatively stable in the adolescent years, again accounting for approximately half the test responses. The data of Levitt and Truumaa are consistent with the Ames data. Ames et al. (1974) suggest an expectancy of 35–50 percent for A% in the adult years. Among elderly subjects, Ames et al. (1973) measured A% to be 46, 55, and 40 percent for normal, presenile, and senile subjects, respectively. There was a slight increase with age, from 52 percent at age 70, to 53 percent at age 80, and 56 percent at age 90. This tendency of A% to increase slightly with age among the elderly was confirmed by longitudinal findings.

Anatomy Responses (At)

Ames et al. (1974) found an average of less than one anatomic response per record through all the childhood age groups except age 9, where the mean was 1.2. "Anatomy responses . . . come inconspicuously at 8, 9, and 10 years, approximating about one response per child at each of these ages. A few girls at 10 years give *only* anatomic responses" (Ames et al., 1974, p. 82). Unfortunately, socioeconomic variables were not considered with respect to the At response. Levitt and Truumaa report a similar finding of less than 1.0. At responses at all ages.

In the adolescent period (Ames et al., 1971) anatomic responses remained fairly static, averaging below 1.0 response per record except at age 14, where the mean was 1.21. Levitt and Truumaa report means below 1.0 for all the adolescent ages.

Among elderly subjects (Ames et al., 1973), a decided increase in anatomy percepts was found with progressive senility; the average responses per record were 0.5, 1.4, and 8.4 for normal, presenile, and senile subjects respectively. In fact, anatomic responses were the most common responses in the records of senile subjects. In contrast, At% decreased with age, from 12 at age 70, to 10 at age 80, and 0 at age 90. This decrease is confirmed by the longitudinal data of Ames et al. (1973). These authors also report that At% increased with decreased socioeconomic status, from 8.16 to 15.79 percent. The institutionalized elderly were also found to have higher At% than the noninstitutionalized subjects—17.63 versus 6.38.

POPULAR RESPONSES

The responses scored popular in the Ames collection of normative studies were specifically chosen using statistical criteria from the test responses of the normative samples. The actual frequencies and percentages thus obtained are, therefore, likely to be of little value to the psychologist who uses other lists of populars. However, the general trends found are worth noting. Ames et al. (1974) found that P% doubled from age 2 to age 10. Levitt and Truumaa also found a substantial increase with age during childhood. Subjects from lower socioeconomic backgrounds in the Ames investigation were generally higher in P% than subjects from the higher social classes. P stayed relatively constant through the adolescent years according to the Ames data (Ames et al., 1971), though Levitt and Truumaa found a slight increase with age. Among the elderly (Ames et al., 1973), the popular score was found to drop from the normal, to the presenile, to the senile subjects. P% does not seem to be related to socioeconomic status among the elderly.

Noninstitutionalized subjects gave significantly more popular responses than did the institutionalized.

RESPONSE TOTAL (R)

Ames et al. (1974) report that for their child subjects, total R showed a tendency to increase during childhood, from a mean of 9.6 at 2 years to 18.6 at 9 years. It should be noted that R was found to be smaller among children from lower socioeconomic backgrounds. Thus, while 9-year-old children from the higher socioeconomic backgrounds displayed a mean of 18.6 total responses, subjects from the inner city displayed a mean of 10 responses. Levitt and Truumaa indicate that R has a slight tendency to increase, from an average of 15.6 at age 5, to 20.8 by age 16. These statistics represent their average and bright groups combined. In the Ames et al. data on adolescents (1971), similar statistics are presented. Ames et al. also note that for the adolescent group, girls typically give a larger number of responses than do boys.

In the Ames et al. data (1973) on elderly subjects, a steady decrease in number of responses with increased deterioration of the subject is noted. Normal subjects gave a mean of 26 responses, preseniles a mean of 16, while seniles gave a mean of only 13 responses. Female subjects tended to give more responses than the male subjects. A consistent drop with age was also seen—subjects in their 70s gave a mean of 19.52 responses, those in their 80s a mean of 15.27 responses, and those in their 90s a mean of 14.98 responses.

7

Introduction to Content Analysis

While Hermann Rorschach and many of his later followers in the United States have tended to deemphasize the importance of the content of Rorschach responses, clinicians have increasingly come to recognize that what the subject reports seeing in the blot constitutes very valuable data. Several studies (Potkay, 1971; Powers & Hamlin, 1957; Symonds, 1955) have demonstrated that clinicians rely heavily on content in arriving at conclusions about test subjects. Furthermore, the accumulated evidence on test validity is generally quite favorable for the various content scales that have been developed (Anastasi, 1976; Aronow & Reznikoff, 1976). In keeping with this increasing recognition of the pivotal importance of inkblot content, the present chapter will discuss the major approaches to such content interpretation.

NOMOTHETIC VERSUS IDIOGRAPHIC INTERPRETATION OF CONTENT

In general, we may distinguish between two primary approaches to Rorschach content interpretation. Consistent with Allport's delineation of the two major types of personality description (Allport, 1937, 1961), these two approaches might be dubbed the nomothetic vs. the idiographic. As noted by Allport, the nomothetic approach to personality description contrasts a particular subject to a comparison group in terms of the degree to which a particular trait or characteristic is present. One is then able to state that a test subject is above or below the mean of a particular comparison group for sets of specific traits, and how far away from the mean his or her score is.

Quite a number of nomethetically-based inkblot content scales have been put forward in recent years, including the Elizur scales of anxiety and hostility (Elizur, 1947), the "homosexual signs" scale (Wheeler, 1949), De Vos' scales of affective inference (De Vos, 1952), scales developed by Zubin and co-workers (Zubin, Eron, & Schumer, 1965), the Barrier and Penetration scales of Fisher and Cleveland (1958/1968), the Endicott scales of depression and suspiciousness (1972), and the Holt content scales of primary process and secondary process (Holt & Havel, 1960). The reader interested in the accumulated empirical evidence bearing on these nomothetic content scales is referred to the appropriate chapters in Aronow and Reznikoff (1976) and to Reznikoff, Aronow, and Rauchway (1982).

In contrast to the nomothetic approach, the idiographic approach to personality description focuses not on those traits or characteristics which are conceptualized as common denominators of everyone's behavior, but, rather, on those aspects of the individual which are unique. A high degree of descriptive specificity thus characterizes the idiographic approach. When the clinician interprets the content of the subject's Rorschach responses from the idiographic perspective, the content is used to portray the subject's highly individual views of him- or herself and his or her environment.

An example of nomothetic versus idiographic content interpretation will help to clarify the distinction that is being made.

A 25-year-old male homosexual psychiatric outpatient reports the following percept on Card I of the Rorschach test:

> Two witches—one on the right, one on the left—and a body in-between them. The witches have their capes and hoods on. They're not seducing her or he— it's like a ritual—a sacrifice.

The patient's associations to this percept were as follows:

> On TV last night—I saw the actress who was in King Kong—that made me think of the girl being sacrificed. (What does this make you think of in your own life?) We all sacrifice—I'm sacrificing my own day just being here—and sometimes we sacrifice in the things we do at work. (What does a witch remind you of?) Evil and good. Most people think they're evil—but who's to say— maybe they do good, too.*

This response would be dealt with from a nomothetic content perspective by scoring it on various content scales—as to whether and to what extent it constituted a response indicating such traits as anxiety, hostility, dependency, suspiciousness, etc. The subject's total scale scores might then be compared with those of other subjects in relevant "comparison groups."

In contrast, the idiographic approach to understanding this response

---

*The method by which such associations to Rorschach percepts are obtained is discussed in Chapter 9.

would focus on such qualitative aspects of the response as the subject's transformation of the witch into someone who may do "good"—perhaps indicating the defense mechanism of denial. Another possible meaning for this particular subject might involve the question of whether he perceived his mother as seductive, and his need to deny it—"they're *not* seducing . . . "). Also notable is his subtle doubt as to the sex of the figure in the middle ("her or he"), perhaps indicating some confusion in sexual identity. Irritation is expressed in the patient's remark about "I'm sacrificing my own day just being here." In short, the content of the patient's response and his highly individual manner of verbalizing, reveals much about his idiographic personality functioning.

Thus, the two primary modes of content interpretation, the nomothetic and the idiographic, produce different types of information about the test subject. The interpretive procedure also is quite different in each case. It could be argued that because the Rorschach test requires the subject alone to provide the structure of the response, a great heterogeneity of content results which allows for the expression of stylistic differences. One might, therefore, expect the responses produced to lend themselves most readily to an analysis of the subject's idiosyncratic views rather than a structured nomothetic assessment of the degree to which particular traits are present. In any event, there is as yet insufficient information on reliability, validity, and norms for the nomothetic content scales; they are not ready for clinical use at this time (Aronow & Reznikoff, 1976; Reznikoff et al., 1982). Their primary use, at present, is for research. The remaining clinical discussion of content will therefore deal entirely with the idiographic mode of content interpretation.

IDIOGRAPHIC CONTENT INTERPRETATION

The idiographic interpretation of the "witch" response summarized above serves to highlight the major aspects of idiographic interpretive technique:

1. Symbolism is central to idiographic content interpretation. Thus, the content of the test response is often assumed to symbolize or stand for an aspect of the test subject's life. The interpretation of Rorschach percepts is similar in this respect to the psychoanalytic interpretation of dreams— both types of interpretation assume that the material to be interpreted may be understood as an expression of the subject's emotional life. However, not all Rorschach percepts can be understood as symbolic expressions that relate to the subject's personality. Rather, the Rorschach response represents something of a blend of symbolic-emotional elements with an objective description of the blots. Thus, the Rorschach clinician must learn to identify those Rorschach responses

which are likely to be particularly revealing of personality and to otherwise disentangle the projective from the nonprojective aspects of particular responses. (This is discussed further in the following chapter.)
2. Idiographic content interpretation often relies heavily on "stylistic analysis" of the subject's response, placing emphasis on verbalizations that may accompany the percept. Thus, in the response noted above, it is not only the content per se that is interpreted, but the subject's idiosyncratic way of expressing and modifying the percept, and also the subject's accompanying associations to the percept.
3. In most cases, conclusive interpretations about the idiographic meaning of particular Rorschach responses and verbalizations are difficult to reach. A particular aspect of the response, in other words, usually "suggests" a particular interpretation. Only if there is a confluence of data from several sources in the test record can the clinician be reasonably confident of the accuracy of interpretations.

INFORMATION PROVIDED BY IDIOGRAPHIC CONTENT INTERPRETATION

In a previous volume (Aronow & Reznikoff, 1976), we summarized our findings regarding the major types of information revealed by test subjects in their inkblot responses. The self-concept is foremost; inkblot responses often serve as a mirror for the individual. How the subject sees him- or herself is often vividly displayed in the test response, particularly with respect to negative aspects of the self-concept. Important others in the subject's life and aspects of the environment that impinge on the test subject are also often highlighted in Rorschach responses. We have found it useful to classify the types of information produced by Rorschach responses into five broad categories.

INFORMATION REVEALED BY RORSCHACH RESPONSES

Self-Concept

The following percept on Card VI, expressed by a 29-year-old depressed female outpatient with a chronic obesity problem, is an example of how self-concept may be revealed:

Card VI: A primitive alimentary canal.
Associations: Makes me think of a worm—what a worm
                       might have. (What does a worm bring to

mind?) Loathing, disgust—and that makes
me think of my own self-hatred—
incompetency—ineffectuality, weakness.

In this response, the patient reveals a very poor self-image and anger directed at the self, connected with her primitive oral needs.

Attitudes Towards
Significant Others in the Environment

The following percept on Card VII was elicited from a 26-year-old male patient hospitalized for depression and paranoid thinking. His response reveals feelings he has about his mother and his environment.

Card VII:	It looks like two young ladies talking to each other.
Associations:	(What does that remind you of?) Nothing much—they have freedom of movement— they're moving their lips. (What does freedom of movement make you think of in your own life?) Anything that stifles movement—like my mother. It's hard for me to express myself with her.

This response expresses the test subject's feeling of restriction at the hands of his mother.

Perceptions of the Environment, Both Social
and Otherwise

This percept, on Card I, was reported by a 24-year-old female patient hospitalized after a suicide attempt. Her impression of her environment is revealing.

Card I:	It could also be an insect.
Associations:	Makes me think of being stung or bitten by an insect—nature is destructive. (What does that bring to mind?) You have to be careful in life—you have to protect yourself. God created a world which is dangerous.

In this response, the patient reveals her view of her environment as malevolent and destructive.

Major Concerns

This is a highly heterogeneous category that involves all manner of external and internal stress with which the ego is attempting to cope. An example is seen in the following response to Card VII by a 23-year-old woman hospitalized with complaints of temper outbursts and bizarre behavior:

Card VII:	It looks like two little children with ponytails—they're on top of pillows. It looks like they're mad at each other—they're up in the air—somebody threw them up—now they're floating down.
Associations:	It's like a decal-decoration for a baby's room—something I'd put on the end of the crib. I went to Woolworth one day, and saw decals like that—something for babies. (What does their being mad remind you of?) They're not exactly angry—just teasing each other. (What does being mad make you think of in your own life?) Nobody exactly was against me—nobody said I have a boyfriend and you don't, I got engaged and you didn't—except my mother—she says my boyfriend and I don't love each other just because we argue. Since I came into the hospital, she doesn't say it anymore—now she says, "your fiancé loves you very much."

In this response and the accompanying associations in particular, the patients reveals a complex of feelings involving stress induced by her relationship with her boyfriend. Other themes touched on here include anger towards both her mother and her boyfriend, her desire for children, feelings of inferiority in relation to other women, and secondary gain aspects of her hospitalization.

Ongoing Conflicts

An example is seen in the following response to Card IX by a bisexual male outpatient with complaints of free-floating anxiety:

Card IX:	It looks like a king and a queen.
Associations:	Reminds me of myself in a way—sometimes going one way sexually, sometimes the other—AC-DC.

This response highlights the subject's split in sexual identity, with some underlying grandiosity also suggested.

The symmetricality of the inkblots is particularly conducive to eliciting such a sense of division in test subjects. When symmetrically identical parts of a blot are described as opposites on some pole, as in this response, a split in the subject's feelings about the self or something external to the self is usually indicated.

The interested reader is referred to our earlier volume for further discussion and examples of these categories of response. The reader should be aware, however, that such categorization of responses, while didactically helpful, does some violence to a true understanding of the meaning of inkblot responses. A particular inkblot response typically combines elements that cut across these categories in a gestalt that is stylistically unique to each subject, reflecting the idiosyncratic manner in which he or she views the self and the environment.

8

Guidelines to Valid Content Interpretation

Because of the requirement that the individual structure his or her own responses on the inkblot task, the Rorschach test is able to provide qualitative information about the test subject which nomothetically-based objective tests cannot possibly elicit. Idiographic content interpretation thus provides the clinician with very valuable information about test subjects. At the same time, however, it must also be recognized that there are major hazards in this type of test interpretation.

As noted by Schafer (1954), the Rorschach percept must be considered distinctly inferior to the dream in terms of its interpretive potential. The inkblot response often represents a blend of the objective blot properties with projective elements. Considerable skill and experience are required to successfully disentangle these elements of the response. The dream, however, typically has no such objective stimulus in the real world. Furthermore, the narrative continuity and autobiographical specificity of the dream render it more suitable than the Rorschach percept for analysis. In addition, the associations obtained by the psychotherapist to the subject's dream provide further valuable data for purposes of interpretation; it is not standard practice, however, to garner associations to Rorschach percepts.*

It also must be recognized that the interpretive context of inkblot testing often further reduces the power of such interpretation, as contrasted with the interpretation of dreams. The Rorschach examiner often has little prior information about the testee's background, personality, and idiosyncratic views of the world. The psychotherapist, in contrast, is intimately familiar with the patient whose dream is to be interpreted and is thus in a favorable

---

*Associative procedures which can be used with the Rorschach test are discussed in Chapter 9.

position to interpret the patient's idiosyncratic use of the symbols. Additionally, the patient can and does correct wrong dream interpretations, whereas this is rarely the case in Rorschach interpretation.

In short, it is difficult to avoid Schafer's conclusion that "insofar as the Rorschach response expresses unconscious, infantile tendencies, it is ordinarily a guidepost to these tendencies and not a highly articulated map of the unconscious terrain" (Schafer, 1954, p. 96). As a tool of less power than the dream, the Rorschach test thus lends itself much more readily to wild symbolic analysis than does the dream. Too often, Rorschach content interpretation deteriorates into "wildly imaginative and highly subjective interpretations which have [served to render] . . . projective techniques more highly projective for the examiner than for the subject" (Anastasi, 1976, p. xi).

RULES FOR VALID CONTENT INTERPRETATION

Given this state of affairs, we have chosen to present a set of 16 guidelines to inkblot content interpretation which should help the clinician avoid wild analysis and maximize the accuracy of interpretations arrived at through the idiosyncratic interpretation of content.

The Conservative Interpretation

The Rorschach clinician must be very conservative in interpreting inkblot content; he should be aware of the instrument's inherent weaknesses. When in doubt as to whether a particular response should be interpreted, the clinician should prefer to err on the side of caution. While clinical sensitivity is clearly an important characteristic for the effective interpretation of content, the Rorschacher must be wary of overconfidence that may lead to unjustified speculation; one must not go beyond the data in arriving at conclusions about test subjects.

The Doubtful Response

As noted by Hertzman and Pearce (1947), it is important for the Rorschacher to be willing to say that he or she does not know the meaning of doubtful responses. When the test record consists largely of such test responses, the psychologist must acknowledge in the psychological report that the psychodynamics of the test subject are not clear (although the defensive style of the subject may be quite evident in the test responses) (See Schafer, 1954).

Responses with Uncertain Referents

As also pointed out by Hertzman and Pearce (1947), the clinician must be particularly wary of interpreting responses whose referents are uncertain. Thus, if a male patient gives the following response to Card VII: "Two women who are crying—feeling sorry for themselves," it is by no means clear whether the patient is referring to himself or to other important figures in his life. While the dynamic inquiry technique presented in Chapter 9 can help to clarify the referents of doubtful responses, the clinician should refrain from interpreting such responses in the absence of clarifying material.

Misuse of "Fixed Meanings"

The Rorschacher should avoid interpretations based primarily on tables of "fixed meaning" for various content categories. As should be clear from our presentation thus far, the psychologist is often in doubt as to the dynamic meaning of many responses. The clinician might thus be tempted to resort to sources such as the "animal list" and associated ego qualities presented by Phillips and Smith (1953). Resorting to tables of fixed meaning for dynamic Rorschach interpretation is no more defensible than the use of "dream books" in the interpretation of dreams. Such categorized treatment of dynamic symbols ignores the highly idiosyncratic nature of symbol usage and is likely to lead to a very high degree of interpretative error.

Over-Reliance on Hypothetical Evocative Qualities

The clinician should avoid interpretations based primarily on assumed card meaning. Many authors have presented hypotheses with regard to particular evocative qualities of Rorschach blots. The most familiar such hypotheses are those which describe Card IV as the "father card," Card VI as the sex card," and Card VII as the "mother card." The research literature on the subject reviewed in our earlier volume (Aronow & Reznikoff, 1976) concluded that the respective hypotheses regarding these cards must be considered doubtful. The clinician who assumes that responses to Card IV invariably reflect on the father, to Card VI on sexuality, and to Card VII on the mother is thus on very shaky ground.

Disentangling the Projective from the Nonprojective

The clinician must be able to disentangle the projective from the nonprojective aspects of the inkblot response. The subject's test response may be regarded as a blend of objective description of and typical reaction to blot properties on the one hand, and projective elements from within the test subject on the other. Extensive clinical experience is, of course, helpful in separating these two elements. A knowledge of common responses elicited by blots and blot areas can help in the teasing apart of the two elements. An awareness of how subjects typically respond to the blots is also useful in this regard.

As noted in Chapter 1, we suggest that one be most reluctant to interpret responses to blots which are in keeping with the blot stimulus properties. Negatively tinged responses to Cards I and IV, for example, should be interpreted with considerable caution since these blots are perceived by most subjects as very negative stimuli. If an emotionally negative response to Card I is obtained, one would thus require more evidence than usual that the response has projective elements and is not merely an appropriate emotional response to the blot stimulus properties.

Knowledge of General Psychodynamics

A firm grasp of general Freudian psychodynamics as well as defensive operations is very helpful to the psychologist engaging in the dynamic interpretations of content. In particular, training and experience in dream interpretation is highly beneficial to the Rorschach clinician. One's own personal analysis or psychotherapy is also likely to be useful in eliminating blind spots and increasing clinical sensitivity.

The Testers Own "Blind Spots"

The clinician should try to be sensitive to cumulative data on his or her own "blind spots" in test interpretation. Thus, if a clinician finds him- or herself describing the dynamics of many diverse test subjects in the same manner (a manner strikingly similar to the tester's own dynamics), it is quite possible that the tester is doing his or her own projecting in the interpretive situation. The opposite type of error (a blindness to certain aspects of psychodynamics) is more difficult for the tester to discover.

Sequence Analysis

The sensitive clinician should interpret responses not as discrete entities but in reference to the surrounding test responses. This aspect of inkblot interpretation, dubbed "sequence analysis" by early Rorschachers, is particularly valuable in dynamic Rorschach work. When a major conflictual theme in the subject's life manages to intrude into a Rorschach response, one often finds a fascinating "ebb and flow" of wish and defense, of ambivalent feelings, and of other related aspects of the subject's personality in the surrounding responses to the same blot and perhaps later in the test protocol. Because of its great importance in projective interpretation, content sequence analysis will be discussed in more detail in Chapter 10.

Characteristics of Heavy Dynamic Loading

The skilled clinician should be aware of those characteristics which identify the response carrying a heavy dynamic loading, Mindess (1970), in particular, has written of the characteristics of revealing Rorschach responses, focusing on four such aspects: originality, emotional cathexis, imaginativeness, and repetition.

Originality

According to Mindess, the more unusual an idea is, the more justified one is in considering it symbolic. Thus, "a bat" seen on Card I is far less likely to be dynamically meaningful than a highly original response such as "the Greek winged victory, a statue of a woman representing freedom."

Emotional Cathexis

The more clearly imbued with emotion a response is, the more likely it is symbolic. Thus, seeing two people on the sides of Card I is less likely to be meaningful than seeing two people tearing a child apart.

Imaginativeness

The more the imagination of the subject is invoked by the percept, the more likely the percept is dynamically meaningful. Mindess presented an example of a highly imaginative response to Card IX: "Vapor shooting up into the air and in the background there are mountains, pure white, and golden gates, carved perfectly, and way back in the distance is a tower and that tower is the capitol of the world and it's so beautiful that it makes everything look bright" (Mindess, 1970, p. 85).

Repetition

Mindess has also suggested that a category of response repeated within the Rorschach record is more likely to be symbolically significant than a response that occurs only once.

The interested reader is referred to Mindess' article for a more detailed description of these response characteristics.

Confluence of Data

The tester should look for a confluence of test data before making statements about the testee. Major trends within the test subject typically manifest themselves repeatedly in the test battery. Sometimes, however, a particularly transparent response will suggest an important dynamic trend that is not confirmed elsewhere in the record. On such occasions, it is usually appropriate to include such interpretations in the test report but to also indicate the tentativeness of them. On the other hand, the tester should also indicate those interpretations in which he or she has a good deal of confidence because evidence to support them occurs throughout the test battery.

Quantitative Judgments Based on Idiographic Analysis

The Rorschacher should avoid quantitative judgments about test subjects based on idiographic analysis. To the extent that the term "measurement" can be applied to idiographic interpretation, it is clearly a very primitive form of measurement, perhaps analogous to what Stevens (1951) has called a "nominal scale," with a one-to-one correspondence assumed to exist between the percepts and the relevant aspects of the subject's personality. This very primitive level of measurement implies that judgments of quantity (e.g., how anxious is the subject based on idiographic interpretation of content) cannot be expected from such data. It may be possible to make more sophisticated quantitative judgments based on nomothetic inkblot content scales, but the very limited reliability and normative data available on most of these scales makes it inadvisable for the clinician to make such Rorschach-based quantitative judgments at this time.

At first blush, this rule would seem to contradict Schafer's (1954) dictum that the psychologist should seek to indicate the intensity of interpreted trends. Although the importance of specifying the degrees to which certain trends are present cannot be denied, such specification requires nomothetic scales with adequate psychometric foundations, notably lacking in the Rorschach Test. The clinician should thus form such quantitative judgments on the basis of appropriate nomothetic instruments.

Comprehensive History of Testee

All else being constant, the greater the knowledge the examiner possesses about the background of the test subject, the more effective will be the idiographic Rorschach interpretation. Given the highly idiosyncratic nature of symbol usage, the psychologist needs as intimate a knowledge of the test subject as it is possible to acquire. Too often, examiners know little or nothing about the histories of the testees, and sometimes even pride themselves on their ability to do "blind analysis." A high degree of interpretive error is likely to result from such blind analysis. We favor the taking of comprehensive histories from subjects as part of the testing process.

Feedback from Others

The competent clinician should augment his clinical expertise by seeking feedback about the accuracy of his test observations from those in a position to render such judgments, most notably psychotherapists who have known the testees over significant periods of time. Such feedback is likely to help identify the tester's "blind spots" in interpretation.

Behavioral Data

The clinician must be alert to relevant behavior demonstrated during testing, behavior which may help the tester arrive at a more meaningful interpretation of responses. Does the subject, for example, display signs of anxiety or agitation in the process of responding (voice breaking, occurrence of tics, profuse sweating, breaking of eye contact, shift of posture, etc.)? Does the subject give blatantly sexual, morbid, gory, or bizarre responses with no sign of concern or emotional involvement? The clinician must regard him- or herself—during the Rorschach administration in particular—as an important clinical instrument for the detection and evaluation of such behavioral data that can help shed light on the dynamic constitution of the subject.

Testee as Partner

Last but not least, the Rorschach testee should be regarded by the examiner as a partner in the testing process rather than a naive individual to be duped into revealing significant material. Leventhal et al. (1962) discussed the potential benefits of the "active handling of the patient-psychologist relationship" extensively (p. 77). Leventhal et al. (1962) have suggested an extensive pretest interview in which the subject is encouraged to collaborate with the examiner to produce a useful test record. The examiner may also wish to use this pretest period for acquiring extensive historical material about the test subject.

In our previous volume (Aronow & Reznikoff, 1976), we suggested that the patient may also be recruited as an active participant in the interpretative process by making major modifications in the Rorschach inquiry procedure. In our experience, patients typically know that the Rorschach test is designed to reveal personality functioning. Once the initial response process is completed, they may then be asked to clarify the meaning of their percepts through an associative procedure and even by means of direct questioning. This modified clinical use of the Rorschach procedure will be discussed in Chapter 9.

9

Content-Oriented Administration Procedures

As noted in Chapter 8, dynamic interpretation of Rorschach responses obtained in the association phase of testing can be quite problematic, often leading to excursions into wild analysis. To help clarify the dynamic meaning of particular Rorschach responses and to counter the problem of wild analysis, a number of altered administration procedures have been proposed in the literature.

The earliest suggestion of modified procedure was put forward by Burt (Note 1). Burt chose to eliminate the standard inquiry procedure and to substitute an inquiry into the source of the percept in the subject's life experience. Unfortunately, Burt did not present the instructions used for his inquiry procedure, nor did he give the reader any idea of how such inquiry is to be conducted.

In contrast, Janis and Janis (1946, 1965) presented a highly structured technique in which free associations are obtained to the Rorschach percepts. The Janis procedure involves standard instructions read to every subject and a procedure wherein chains of associations are obtained. Kessel, Harris, and Slagle (1969) also suggested the use of associations in clarifying the dynamic meaning of content.

Several authors have recommended other techniques for obtaining more dynamic information from the Rorschach test. Appelbaum (1959, 1965) suggested changing the atmosphere in which the test is administered, with the examiner indicating by his behavior that the formal test session is over after the Rorschach is administered. The subject is then asked in an "informal" manner to go through the cards again and to indicate if he or she sees anything else. Kornrich (1965) also suggested a "second run" through the blots to elicit new responses.

Halpern (1957, 1965) advocates a procedure wherein the examiner, in a post-test session, tries to validate his or her Rorschach-based hypotheses by directly questioning the subject about his or her personality. Leventhal et al. (1962) suggested an "active handling of the patient–psychologist relationship," with an extensive pretest interview to establish a collaborative relationship with the examiner, and with the testing itself turned into a combination of test and interview procedure.

Arthur (1965) presented the only altered Rorschach procedure designed primarily for children. Arthur's technique is suitable for use with children who produce barren or constricted records. Arthur essentially asks her subjects questions that elicit thematic material. Thus, the subject is gradually required to construct a story around the percept.

Elitzur (1976) introduced an "imaginary story and self-interpretation" technique for use in Rorschach content analysis. Following the traditional inquiry, Elitzur has his subjects use each of the percepts as the main theme for an imaginary story. Subjects are then told that the stories should reflect what they are experiencing inwardly, and they are asked to identify with the characters of the story. The subjects' responses to the procedures are then interpreted from a Gestalt perspective.

A more complete description of many of the procedures summarized above can be found in our previous book (Aronow & Reznikoff, 1976). None of these procedures have been adopted by clinicians to any great extent, in part, because they typically involve additional testing time requirements. We have therefore developed what we call the Content Rorschach Technique, which substitutes a content-oriented inquiry for the traditional inquiry procedure, similar to what was initially suggested by Burt (Note 1).

THE CONTENT RORSCHACH TECHNIQUE

In the Content Rorschach Technique, the association phase of the Rorschach is first administered, using the standard instructions as presented in Chapter 1. After the subject has given response(s) to Card I, he or she is told, "Now I'd like you to show me where you saw these things on the blot. Where is the _____ you saw?" Locations are thus obtained with the help of a standard location sheet following each blot during this first phase of testing. This is done to ensure that the inquiry period may be devoted entirely to dynamic associations.

Following the completion of the first phase of testing with all 10 blots, subjects are then presented with the following instructions:

> There's one more part to this test. Sometimes what people see in the cards brings to mind something that they remember, either recently or a long time ago, or makes them think of something. When I read back your responses to you, I'd like you to tell me the first thing that comes to mind.

After the subject's first association to these instructions, further associations may be elicited if the data warrant it. The subject may then be asked to associate to his or her associations, as in the Janis procedure; the subject may be asked to associate to a particular part of the percept, or the subject may be asked to respond to combinations of percepts, and the subject may even be asked to relate the percept to his or her own life. In other words, at this point, the Rorschach is no longer a standard procedure; the examiner may direct the subject's verbalizations in any way which seems likely to lead to clinically meaningful information.

An example of the use of our inquiry technique will serve to further clarify the nature of our technique. A 23-year-old woman who was hospitalized following a suicide attempt gave the following response on Card III: "Two butlers preparing a meal." When Card III was reached in the second phase of testing, the subject was read her response and was asked what it made her think of. She replied, "Just two butlers preparing pancakes or something." She was then asked what preparing pancakes reminded her of (since this was the new element she introduced in her association). She then replied, "Now it reminds me of something very silly—my father and mother used to argue over who used to make the better pancakes." (What does that call to mind?) "It was a very silly fight—all you could do was laugh at them. My sister said my father's were better, so I always said my mother's were better."

In this chain of verbalizations, several dynamic elements are revealed, including parental conflict over oral supplies, denigration of the parents, a split of alliances in her family of childhood, and rivalry with her sister.

The questioning technique that we have found to be most helpful has several characteristics:

1. The questions asked are open-ended—subjects are asked what something makes them think of, reminds them of, etc. There is as little focus as possible to these questions, thus maintaining the amorphous, projective nature of the task. We typically vary the wording of such questions so as to avoid sterotyped repetition: thus, such phrases as, "What does _____ make you think of," "What does _____ call to mind," "What does that bring to mind," are used.

2. The examiner has great freedom in terms of choosing the direction in which he or she wants the procedure to continue. Thus, in the above example, the examiner chose to respond to the new element (the pancakes) introduced in the patient's initial association. Some other possibilities might be to direct associations to a particular element (in the example, the examiner might have asked what butlers made the subject think of), or to link together more than one response for associative purposes (e.g., the subject might be asked what this resposne and another taken together called to mind).

3. If the subject does not tacitly acknowledge self-revealing aspects of his
    or her responses, we will for several responses ask the subject directly,
    "What might your seeing _____ in the inkblot reflect about your
    own life?" Such a questioning procedure leads many subjects to reveal
    important dynamic material in this part of the testing. When subjects do
    not respond to this questioning technique, the defensiveness and/or lack
    of psychological mindedness of the test subject constitutes important
    clinical data.

4. At times, the subject's associations to inkblot responses lead to the
    subject speaking of important emotional subjects. At the examiner's
    discretion, the Rorschach testing may then be interrupted to pursue (by
    means of a direct interview) the emotional material that has been
    dredged up by means of the test. Testing may then resume again
    following the brief interview.

5. If the examiner is pressed for time or, if the subject is not responding with
    associations of clinical value, it is not necessary to obtain associations to
    all percepts in the test record. Since the locations have already been
    ascertained in the first phase of testing, scoring and tabulation are still
    possible.

When the Content Rorschach Technique is used in place of the
traditional administration method, there are two major differences in scoring
and tabulation. Firstly, it is no longer possible to score the determinant
category; also, the scoring of Form-Level is modified. Form-Level must now
be scored for all responses that can be said to have a definite form. Thus, a
response on Card X, "a big hooray," would not be scored for Form-Level,
nor would a response on Card VIII, "a chunk of meat," since a chunk of meat
may have any shape at all. The Rorschach summary and tabulation sheets
discussed in Chapter 5 may be used with the Content Rorschach Technique
with the determinant column left blank on the summary sheets, and the
determinant totals and ratios omitted on the tabulation sheet. A protocol
obtained by means of the Content Rorschach Technique is presented in
Chapter 12.

10

Content Sequence Analysis

Many authors have written on the importance of structural sequence analysis in Rorschach interpretation, i.e., viewing responses not in isolation, but in the context of, for example, the types of location areas and determinants occurring chronologically in the total test record (e.g., Beck, Beck, Levitt, & Molish, 1961; Exner, 1974; Klopfer et al., 1954; also, see Chapter 5 in the present text). Such considerations also apply to content interpretation of the Rorschach record. Similarly, when seen from a content perspective, no response stands alone—all must be understood in the larger context of the complete test record.

Because each person is unique, the chronological patterning of responses in each Rorschach record is likewise unique, and the variation in the sequence analysis, which must then be carried out, is consequently enormous. Nonetheless, there are certain general sequence analysis issues which, though they may be manifested differently in diverse Rorschach records, do seem to have commonality as regards content sequence analysis in many test protocols. We, in particular, see five issues to which the Rorschach student should be alert.

REPETITION OF A THEME TO THE
SAME INKBLOT

The repetition of a theme in responses to the *same* inkblot may imply that the theme is of some importance to the subject.

An example of this is seen in the following three responses to Card II by a 24-year-old girl who had been admitted to a psychiatric hospital because of a suicide attempt, and who subsequently had been diagnosed paranoid schizophrenic.

II. 2″ 1. Two old women having a coffee klatsh.	II. 1. They have their cups raised—they're talking. (About what?) Gossiping. (Remind you of?) When I was a little girl—my mother was born in Germany—she and her friend would go into the kitchen, and talk in German—I'd never know what they would talk about. (Makes you think of?) Mixed feelings—glad she wasn't bothering me—but she wasn't there when I wanted to bother her.
II. 2. Two soldiers making a blood pact.	II. 2. This part could be a fur cape, the blood here—their hands are raised in a position where they could be making themselves blood brothers. (Make you think of?) It comes from what happened to me last week—when I felt that the man who hypnotized me made a blood pact with a group that called themselves the black scorpions—I D.K. if it was real or in my head. (Remind you of?) Slitting my wrists—slitting the flesh in some way, letting blood.
II. 3. Two dogs looking out of the window, and seeing two people fighting outside. That's all.	II. 3. The two upper red things are people fighting. (Remind you of?) My sister and I watching my mother and her friend in the kitchen—feeling closed out. (Think of then?) Alienation—the window represents the fact they were speaking German.

In the first and third responses, we have a repetition of the theme of emotional distance and alienation from the mother. In the middle response, we find a reference to paranoid ideation and her recent suicide attempt. This might suggest a pivotal importance of this patient's experience of alienation and emotional distance in her childhood and a possible linkage to her subsequent emotional development and symptomatology.

REPETITION OF A THEME TO DIFFERENT INKBLOTS

The repetition of a theme in response to *different* inkblots might similarly imply that the theme is of importance to the subject. An example of such repetition of theme on different blots can be seen in the following responses of a 21-year-old white male hospitalized because of a schizo-phrenic break.

I. It looks like a—oh boy. It looks like—oh boy. 38" 1. It looks like two people dancing.

I. 1. I first saw it as a coat—maybe two people locked together—maybe my mother and I locked together on an unconscious basis—two people, separate yet together.

II. 4" 1. It looks like two lambs sucking on some milk.

II. 1. Reminds me of my mother's operation—she had her breasts removed—and I felt very depressed, forlorn, and lost.

III. 3" 1. Two people sitting opposite each other.

III. 1. I saw a program once on someone who was throwing a violin. My mother is using the strings—of my own instrument. The smudge is how I'm carrying myself. Beauty isn't coming out of the music maker.

These responses largely speak for themselves in terms of the symbiotic, destructive relationship between this patient and his mother, and his intense hostility towards the mother. The extent to which similar associations suffuse his test record points to the crucial nature of his relationship with his mother.

THE SHIFT BETWEEN WISH AND DEFENSE

The ebb and flow of the shift between wish and defense can often be seen in the sequencing of Rorschach response content. A good example of this is revealed in the following responses of a 35-year-old female psychiatric inpatient.

II. 6" 1. Two Folies Bergere type women—they're all made up—they're putting their hands together, with black and red costumes—they're sort of dancing.

II. 1. I'm an entertainer—I like to be on stage—I'm basically an exhibitionist—I like to get attention.

II. 2. It looks like a butterfly—but the butterfly has two sharp claws coming out. It

II. 2. I always loved butterflies—they're such delicate, pretty things. But this is a dangerous butterfly.

would be a pretty
butterfly, except for
the two claws.

II. 3. There's also an
urn in the middle.
Now the two women
look like they're half
animal and half
women—their feet
look like bears feet. I
don't like them.

In this series of responses and associations, one sees the shift from the decorative-passive feminine percept (Folies Bergere-type women), continued in the butterfly image, with the aggressive-hostile wishes then emerging to complicate the percept and the self-concept (dangerous butterfly with sharp claws). There is an attempt at recovery with a feminine-receptive percept (the urn), but the defensive recovery is unsuccessful, with the initial percept then complicated by the introduction of aggressive drive material (the Folies Bergere women now become half women and half animal, with the patient having an unpleasant reaction to this material).

ADEQUACY OF DEFENSES/DEFENSE OF REPRESSION

By viewing the sequence of the responses in terms of their content, one may see not only the shift between wish and defense, but also the general adequacy of the defenses, particularly with respect to the defense of repression. This is vividly seen in the responses to Card III of the same 21-year-old schizophrenic patient whose responses were reported above.

III. 3″ 1. Two people sitting opposite each other.

III. 1. It seems scary—it looks like men facing each other, holding down women's heads in the water. I once had a roommate who I trusted—he misled me. My whole life could be reversing—it could be me killing my mother.

III. 2. Someone's chest cavity—their lungs.

III. 2. The breathing of life. It also makes me think of my mother's breasts being removed.

III. 3. Someone's asshole.

III. 3. The pleasure of releasing myself, the sides look like buttocks, with the asshole here.

In this progression of three responses, one sees the deterioration of the defenses: the patient begins with fairly socialized and appropriate content (the popular human response), then goes to an internal anatomy response, and finally regresses to a primitive anal response as the defense of repression fails him.

SHIFTS IN FEELING TOWARDS PERSONS AND TOPICS

By the analysis of the sequence and general context of Rorschach responses, one can see shifts in subjects' feelings about a particular person or topic. An example of this is indicated in the following ordering of responses and associations of a 19-year-old female psychiatric outpatient with complaints of anxiety attacks.

IV. 7″ 1. A big grizzly bear—looking up at him from the ground.

IV. 1. It makes me think of my father—he's very tall and very domineering—it's like he's overpowering. (What does that bring to mind?) Anger at times—it's hard to fight back, although I'm starting to be able to tell him how I feel about things. He wanted me to go to Europe with him on a trip, but I realized that I didn't have to, and I told him so.

V. 15″ 1. It looks like some kind of a bug.

V. 1. It makes me think of something that bugs you. (What does that remind you of?) People being on your back about things. (What does that make you think of in your own life?) My boyfriend being on my back lots of times—usually about my moods. But, then, sometimes, he's very understanding.

V. 2. These are like animals—head and one foot of a horse. Like racing on a racetrack.

V. 2. My boyfriend and I went to the racetrack—I liked it, but I'm afraid that he may get into gambling.

V. 3. A man figure with a big nose, the figure of a person.

V. 3. He looks like half man, and half animal. (What does that call to mind?) Maybe my boyfriend. (?) He's watching over me, which makes me feel comfortable—it's really in my best interest. On the other hand, I sometimes get mad, I feel like he's telling me what to do.

In this series of responses on several blots, the patient sketches for us her conflicted relationship with her father and, now, her boyfriend: enjoying the dependency, but resenting the domination.

A different sort of shift is seen in the content of this same patient's responses and associations to Card VIII.

VIII. 10″ 1. These look like bears.	VIII. 1. They could represent like a struggle—in my life—what's happening to me—hoping that I can live a normal life, and feel well.
VIII. 2. It also looks like a sea—as though looking from the moon down.	VIII. 2. I like water—it's cool and soothing. It's a place of tranquility, to get away to. The moon has an effect on the tides, and maybe on your moods.

In these two brief responses, we see the alternation between her sense of internal conflict and her desire for tranquillity and peace.

It should be noted that the content test record included in Chapter 12 of this text likewise demonstrates principles of content sequence analysis.

11

Report Writing

GENERAL CONSIDERATIONS

Report writing is perhaps the most difficult aspect of psychodiagnostic activity for even the more experienced psychologist. Rorschach test interpretations are highly complex and inferential; organizing and integrating them so they can be communicated in a meaningful fashion is sometimes a task of near monumental proportions. This chapter will endeavor to highlight some critical aspects of report writing. For a more comprehensive treatment of the subject, the reader is referred to books by Huber (1961), Walter Klopfer (1960), and Tallent (1975). While specific features of the Rorschach report, as such will be addressed, it is to be recognized that ordinarily the Rorschach is included in a battery of psychological tests yielding more extensive test data. The principles of synthesizing and communicating the findings are essentially the same whether one or more psychological tests are administered.

The most frequent and serious difficulty in Rorschach reports results from the writer loosing sight of the fact that he or she is evaluating a particular person and, instead, becoming immersed in a welter of technical Rorschach details. Dwelling on the various percentages and ratios found in a Rorschach summary table is worse than useless. If an individual who is comparatively unfamiliar with the Rorschach reads this type of report, he or she would not only find it patently incomprehensible, but would very likely regard it as an exercise in obfuscating self-puffery calculated to display the erudition of the writer.

Almost equally disruptive to a reader is a Rorschach report that directs minimal attention to the referring questions and instead launches into a host of issues tangential or unrelated to why the patient was referred for assessment. For example, if the principal referral question asked was whether organicity is present, then writing a report that focuses essentially on the patient's psychosexual adjustment is obviously not very helpful. Of course, very often referral questions are vague or nonexistent and the psychologist, by default, must decide what to include in the report. If the psychologist typically receives such referrals, it is most strongly recommended that he or she educate the referring agent with respect to framing specific referral questions in the context of information which the Rorschach and other psychological tests can realistically provide.

Some referents have the misapprehension that all background information about a client should be withheld from the examiner and that the Rorschach report should be a "blind diagnosis." The rationale behind this is that having other data of various types about the client establishes preconceptions which then serve to color and possibly distort subsequent Rorschach interpretations. While there is doubtlessly some element of truth in this, not having full information about the client creates a much greater potential for misinterpretation. Such variables as education and occupation are critical in providing a meaningful context for interpreting a Rorschach protocol. Other facts in the patient's history might be of equal importance—a recent loss of a loved one, for example. Thus all relevant information about the client who is being assessed should be available to the psychologist when the psychological evaluation is undertaken. Of course, this does not mean that such data should be indiscriminantly regurgitated in a psychological report, especially when it can be obtained in other readily accessible records.

Behavioral observations during the test sessions are as important as the Rorschach responses themselves in drawing a meaningful personality picture of the client. Such observations should be included in a separate introductory section of the report and, wherever pertinent, integrated in the body of the report. A problem sometimes arises when one tries to reconcile general test behavior and the actual Rorschact percepts. An example of this may be an individual who comes to the testing situation and acts in a very diffident passive-compliant manner, but produces Rorschach associations which are rife with aggressive and rebellious elements. Such an incongruity is likely to be spurious rather than real and explainable on the basis of the different levels on which the person functions. In the illustration cited above, the individual's passive submissiveness may result from defensive efforts to deal with unacceptable guilt-producing, angry, destructive thoughts and feelings.

A neophyte Rorschach worker may be greatly discomforted by Rorschach percepts which ostensibly do not seem to fit with behavioral impressions. With further Rorschach experience, however, the psychologist will grow considerably more adept in understanding the interplay between behavior and inner living.

It must be recognized that the psychologist preparing a Rorschach report is working with complex hypotheses and suppositions about personality structure which, in turn, are derived from a set of inferences about the inkblot percepts, as such. This conjectural framework may result in a good deal of hedging and qualifying on the part of the report writer with the assessment abounding in words like "might be," "seems to," "suggests, " etc., and sometimes reliance upon what has been characterized as the "Barnum effect." The "Barnum effect" derives from P.T. Barnum's assertion that "a sucker is born every minute." In terms of report writing, it means in the inclusion of very general interpretations which virtually anyone would regard as essentially descriptive of them. An example of this type of interpretation might be, "the client evidences conflicts."

Avoiding more definitive and specific interpretations at any cost is hardly likely to leave the reader with a sense of confidence about the findings. The writer of the report should try to give key statements in the workup a kind of "level of confidence rating." Thus, when there is a great deal of test data to support a given assertion, this might be indicated by a statement such as, "there is strong evidence of. . . . " On the other hand, if the test protocol contains somewhat minimal or contradictory indications to corroborate an interpretation, then the statement could be prefaced with, "there is some suggestion of. . . . " Occasional interpretations based on slender evidence that help to clarify certain psychodiagnostic aspects are not inappropriate in a report, as long as the referent is made aware of their problematic nature.

The comparatively inexperienced psychologist attempting to interpret the Rorschach often feels a bit bewildered by the plethora of personality data and, therefore, may cling to a "cookbook approach" to interpretation, mechanically looking up given ratios and percentages in a Rorschach textbook and paraphrasing the general interpretations assigned to them. This invariably makes for a highly fragmented, stereotyped report in which the person who has been evaluated frequently gets lost in the course of presenting the test materials. To be at all meaningful, a report must be "person-centered" rather than "test-centered." With additional testing experience accompanied by good supervision and feedback, the psychologist naturally grows more confident and is usually willing to abandon a majority of cookbook interpretations, focusing instead on the unique constellation of personality features of the individual as they emerge on the Rorschach and other tests.

Documentation, that is, citing various ratios or other technical aspects of the psychogram, has no place in the body of a psychological report, except in the learning context. It is presumed that the referring agent is retaining a competent professional with sufficient expertise not to be called upon to "defend" his conclusions. Including scoring or tabulation details of a Rorschach in a report serves more as a disruption than an aid in communicating what is being presented. On the other hand, there are times when the content of the client's own words dramatically capture what the interpreter is trying to convey. To illustrate this, a woman whose Rorschach indicated that she was just barely beginning to emerge from a severe depression, gave the following response to Card IV: "It looks like a dead old tree stump but here at the top a few little green shoots seem to be coming out." To the outer blue details of Card IX, a man whose Rorschach indicated that he experienced life as very unstable and directionless said: "An amoeba constantly changing its shape." In such situations, it might be helpful to quote the material verbatim in the report.

A question which sometimes arises with respect to the Rorschach is whether the psychologist working with it must be totally conversant with a personality theory in order to write good reports. This is perhaps best answered by stating that there certainly must be a capacity for viewing behavior within some conceptual frame of reference, though this need not be in terms of one highly developed and specific personality theory. Flexibility may well be the best posture with regard to theory. Some understanding of theoretical underpinnings of personality is doubtless necessary to integrate various components of a Rorschach protocol in report form. At the same time, being rigidly committed to a particular personality theory may result in procrustean report writing, with all patients arbitrarily squeezed into a fixed theoretic model.

It is worth mentioning that many reports suffer from an overemphasis on symptoms and pathology and dwell only to a minimal extent, if at all, on assets and strengths. It clearly is far easier to delineate the flawed aspects of personality than to identify those which signify at least some modicum of health, especially when a client is in the throes of significant emotional difficulties or on the brink of psychiatric hospitalization. Even the most emotionally disturbed, chronically ill individual has some areas of strength, although these may be very circumscribed and not at all obvious. A careful identification and description of such assets should form an essential portion of the report, especially from the standpoint of assisting in treatment planning.

Whenever possible, the Rorschach should not be administered alone but rather in conjunction with other psychological tests. A test battery usually makes the job of report writing far simpler. Results obtained from one personality test can amplify and complement the data on another. If the tests run the gamut from structuredness to relative unstructuredness, and also tap various levels of conscious control, some very interesting contrasts can be established. Having the Sentence Completion Test and the Rorschach in the same battery, for example, with the former being far more subject to the client's censorship, permits the examiner to gain considerable insight into the client's defensive operations. When an intelligence scale is included in a test battery with the Rorschach, the psychologist is able to compare how the client utilizes his or her intellectual resources in familiar versus less familiar and well-defined situations.

THE WRITING OF THE REPORT

What will be offered in this section of the chapter will be an approach to the actual writing of the report. Various other authors have presented outlines on this subject which are doubtlessly of equal merit. Furthermore, sometimes an institutional or agency setting requires a particular type of report with the inclusion of specific interpretive material. As a consequence, the psychologist working in such a setting may have to comply with the report writing demands of his or her position.

This outline emphasizes the Rorschach rather than psychological reports based on a more extensive battery. As alluded to earlier, however, the principles are essentially the same.

Any approach to report writing should be prefaced with the strong recommendation that considerably more time be devoted to thinking through what is to be put in the report than to the actual writing. Also, apart from the formal content of the report as such, the writer must attend very carefully to the matters of syntax, vocabulary, and punctuation. A report which is ungrammatical, no matter how insightful, will lose some of its value. Continuity is also an exceedingly important aspect of report writing. A logical sequence of ideas must be reflected in the manner in which the interpretive material is presented. The usefulness of report writing is significantly diluted when it is written in a rambling, desultory fashion, skipping from area to area with insufficient attention to continuity.

In most cases, an outline of some type is helpful in formulating a case and organizing the report. If a battery of psychological tests is administered, then the kind of report that discusses each of the tests one at a time should be scrupulously avoided. This type of report is typically rife with redundancy and lacking in meaningful cohesiveness.

What follows is an outline for the content and organization of a Rorschach report. In no sense is this outline meant to be used in all instances. There may be clients who produce Rorschachs yielding little information on some of the areas covered in this outline. On the other hand, the outline is not intended to be all-inclusive, and there may be some Rorschach findings that do not readily fall into any one area.

History and Background Information

This section should succinctly summarize the background history of the test subject that is relevant for the particular testing situation. It should be relatively brief and should not, for example, rephrase information readily available in the social work summary found in the client's folder.

Behavioral Observations

The behavioral observation section describes the major dimensions of the client's behavior during the test session. Just as the name implies, the behavior should be reported at an observational-descriptive level, rather than an interpretive one. Typically included in such a section is a description of the client's appearance and the reason the individual states he or she has been referred for psychodiagnostic evaluation. It is often very helpful to highlight changes that may take place in the client's behavior as the testing session progresses.

Interpretation of Test Findings

This section of the report should provide a coherent survey of what the examiner is able to glean from the test responses, with the following principal areas covered.

Intellectual Components of Personality

This would include any evidence of intellectual impairment; covering intellectual efficiency and potential, the way the client seems to meet practical problems, as well as his or her abstract reasoning ability. Also important would be an assessment of conventional thinking and, by contrast, the capacity to form original ideas. Level of aspiration and range of interests are also to be included, as well as some assessment of intellectual ties with reality.

The Emotional Aspects of Personality

Subsumed under this area is a general evaluation of the client's inner resources, drives, controls over such drives, affective conflicts, degree and type of reactivity to emotional stimuli, mood state, presence of anxiety, and an estimate of the appropriateness of responses to emotional stimuli.

Concept of Self

This portion of the report evaluates how critically and realistically the self is regarded. Is the individual inclined to be inordinately expansive, for example, or are there unwarranted propensities for self-derogation? The concept the individual has of his or her psychosexual role and the amount of introspectiveness and self-understanding manifested are also to be included.

Interpersonal Relations

This section would tap attitudes toward males and females of different ages and in a variety of roles. It covers group identification, general comfortableness in dealing with others, and the types of interactions that are likely to take place within a social context.

Diagnostic Aspects

At the outset, it should be mentioned that the writer of a report is probably best advised to think in terms of a more general diagnostic formulation rather than a diagnostic label such as found in DSM III. A label is a kind of shorthand that is readily understood by professionals in the field; it communicates a considerable amount of information about an individual being assessed in parsimonious fashion. Labeling, however, makes for stereotyping and undercuts the interplay between an individual's basic personality structure and the pathology present. In formulating a diagnostic statement, amount and type of anxiety should be addressed. Reality appreciation should be carefully evaluated; there should be a thorough assessment of the kinds of defense mechanisms operating and their effectiveness in dealing with anxiety and the demands of the environment. It is important that as much or more attention be directed toward the individual's assets as to his maladaptive patterns of behavior.

Prognostic Evaluation

This involves an overall assessment of the individual's strengths and weaknesses, and an estimate of the adequacy of controls, reality testing, and motivation for self-growth.

Summary and Recommendations

This section should review the salient features of the report in succinct fashion, and state recommendations where relevant. Not infrequently, statements about personality not found in the report proper are included in the summary. This is inappropriate. No new material should be included in a summary.

Thus, the writing of a Rorschach report is clearly a formidable task that demands the investment of much energy and effort. It is not enough that one may be the most skilled and perceptive Rorschach tester—one must be capable of incorporating and communicating findings in a written report that provides a comprehensible and informative personality assessment of the client. Sample reports are included with test protocols in Chapter 12.

Sample Protocols

The following two Rorschach protocols include summary, tabulation, and location sheets. The first protocol was obtained by the traditional inquiry technique, with scoring of determinants thus possible. The latter protocol was obtained with the Rorschach Content Technique (see Chapter 9). The two protocols also differ in that the former is from an intact individual who served as a volunteer subject, while the latter protocol was gotten from a schizophrenic outpatient; the latter protocol was also part of a larger test battery. However, interpretations derived from the other tests, with the exception of the WAIS, have been deleted from the report on the second test protocol. Test reports for each follow the Rorschach protocols.

Because of the context of the testing, there is no history and background information section in the first test report. For didactic purposes, the origin of interpretations is indicated in parentheses in both reports, but under normal circumstances in a clinical, school, or other applied setting, such material would not be included in the test report.

Much appreciation is expressed to Betti Schleyer, M.A. of Fordham University who provided the first Rorschach protocol and report in this chapter.

Protocol #1

Rorschach Response Form for Linda; 38 Years Old; 10/19/79

	Response	Inquiry	Loc.	Det.	Cont.	FQ
I. 10″ 1.	Well, of course, it's obviously a bf.	1. (a) The bf was the whole thing. (b) The middle part is the body and these are the wings. These would be markings on the wings.	W(S)	F	A	+ P
2.	Two hands reaching out on top	2. (a) Up here were the hands.	d	M	Hd	+
3.	A Halloween mask almost like a cat—its eyes and mouth are elongated, pulled out.	3. This was the cat—here are the ears, eyes, nose—the whole thing.	W(S)	F	(Ad)	+
4.	∨ I must have Halloween on my mind—I see the mask again—the ears of the cat are at the top. I don't see much more.	4. These would be the eyes—it's more menacing upside down.	W(S)	Fm	(Ad)	+
		A1. It almost ll a pumpkin. (a) The whole thing.	W(S)	F	(Hd)	+
II. 5″ 1.	I see a pretty bf at the bottom—delicate looking.	1. Down here is the bf. (What about it made it look delicate?) The parts of it that seem to fall out from the main body—it wasn't just chunky.	D	F	A	+ P
2.	The middle section almost reminds me of a spaceship.	2. The middle section was the spaceship. This line indicated the part that would come off, the capsule—here's the nose of it.	S	F	Spaceship	+

(continued)

			Loc	Determinant	Content	Form
3.	These two sections 11 two dancing bears holding something in the middle like a candle ∨>∧ that's it.	3. Here were the bears—they're holding something in the middle like a torch or a candle. (b) They looked furry to me and blobby—here's the front leg and the back.	W	Fm·Fc A		+ P
		A1. Here on the (location) chart without any color I see a tiger mask—here are the eyes with the pupils, here's the mouth, jowls, but I don't see it on the card with color.	W	F	(Ad)	+
III. 5" 1.	I see 2 waiters in a restaurant all dressed up in tuxedoes carrying st. They 11 sophisticated, elegant people—almost as if they were putting a tablecloth on a table together.	1. Seemed to be like somebody you'd see in a restaurant. Their getup looked elegant to me—like they're putting st on a table.	W	M	H	+ P
2.	∨ (laughed) I see 2 Africans—1 African because they have large skulls—back to back—doing a dance because 1 foot is up in the air. I don't see the red things as part of it but they're there.	2. They're here—this is 1 foot and the other foot is kicking up in the air—they look African because of the elongated head. They seem to have beards and hair.	W	M	H	+
IV. 13" 1.	I don't see anything right off. This is a very menacing picture—it almost 11 some kind of monster with padded feet and hands.	1. The whole thing was the monster. (What do you mean by "padded"?) This is all furry and this is more like the paws of a bear—his feet are very large so they just kind of plod around (demonstrates with hands).	W	M·Fc	(A)	+
2.	∨ upside down it 11 a leaf when the leaves are turned over—the underside	2. Like a geranium leaf, a very textured leaf—it has variations in the green	W	Fc	Plant	+

doesn't connote beauty because it is dark and isn't that graceful.

	like the shading here, like when a leaf turns over like when it's going to rain. The bottom is a lighter color than the rest of the leaf—this part is the turned over part.				
3. ∨ stem of a plant ∨	3. This part here. (b) Just the general shape.	D	F	Plant	+
V. 8″ 1. a bat—isn't very appealing >∨ I don't have any response to this, 11 a bat. I don't see anything else.	1. The whole thing was the bat. (b) The different parts 11 a bat. (c) It's just there.	W	F	A	+ P
VI. 12″ 1. 11 a skin of an animal that you put down as a rug on the floor.	1. I don't remember—like a bearskin rug, just take this part off. Here is the head, paws, hind parts. (b) Just the shape	W	F	A_obj	+ P
2. >∨ I see at the top st like reaching out like the first card—it's all part of the object but yet they're going beyond the limits of the object—going beyond what's there, reaching out.	2. It looks more like hands on Card I—belonging to it but going beyond it.	de	M	(Hd)	+
3. ∧ You can see some sort of totem pole at the top—you have a face and arms sticking out. This section doesn't seem to belong to the rest of the card—it's more graceful.	3. The top part 11 a totem pole.	D	F	(H)	+

(continued)

Card	Response	Inquiry	Loc	Det	Content	P
VII. 6" 1.	11 2 women facing each other with a feather sticking up out of their heads—almost as if one was mimicking the other. They're connected, they're wearing a muff.	1. This was the face and the feather—11 they are mimicking each other, almost like their faces are straining forward.	W	M	H	+ P
2.	The second section 11 a gargoyle with a horn in the front of their head and you can see the eye and nose.	2. This section here is the gargoyle—here's the eye, nose, mouth, horn—11 st you'd find on an old building carved in stone.	D	Fc	(H)	+
3.	>√ . . . the gargoyles upside down 11 elephants' heads w trunks but as a whole I don't see anything	3. Upside down these were the elephants.	D	F	A	+
4.	but the white section 11 the top of a decanter where you have the head and going into the bottle.	4. This was the decanter—this is the top and here's the bottle (b) just the general shape of it	S	F	Obj	+
VIII. 20" 1.	Oh, color. I immediately c 2 rodent animals on either side connected to the mess in the middle but I can't make much of the middle.	1. These 2 here were rodent-type animals.	D→W	F	A	+ P
2.	√ I don't know. The only other thing is the middle section 11 somebody's backbone w vertebrae coming out of it—I don't get much else out of it.	2. Here are the vertebrae, the spinal cord and the vertebrae coming off it.	D(S)	F	At	+ P
IX. 24" 1.	The section at the top sort of rm of that painting of the unicorn in the Met—the way it almost seems suspended in air as if it were a horse and there were feet dancing up in the air.	1. The top section reminded me of the unicorn (b) It's a horse-like animal, its feet are up in the air flailing—it's like some force is holding it suspended in the air.	D	FM·Fm (A)		+

	Location	Determinant	Content	
2. ✓Upside down the orange sections 11 lobsters. The colors are pleasing to me.	2. Upside down it 11 lobsters—these would be feet and maybe coloring 2.	D	FC	A	+

Response	Inquiry	Location	Determinant	Content	Score
2. ✓Upside down the orange sections 11 lobsters. The colors are pleasing to me.	2. Upside down it 11 lobsters—these would be feet and maybe coloring 2.	D	FC	A	+
3. It 11 the green with these fingers on the bottom is reaching out to the pink or wanting to include it in some way.	3. These things down here were the fingers—11 they were trying to include the pink. Other than that the colors are artistic. I don't c anything else.	D	M	Hd	+
X. 5" 1. A very busy picture—I almost automatically think of spring and flowers, birds, gardens, and bugs.	1. This is what reminded me of spring. Everything is placed as though it were delicate and light—floating.	W	Fm	Nature	+
2. These 2 brown things 11 beetles.	2. These things remind me of brown bugs.	D	FC	A	+
3. The yellow reminds me of birds.	3. All 4 were birds, kind of floating around (b) the shape and color and position.	D	FC	A	+
4. The blue reminds me of spiders, friendly spiders. I wouldn't mind having them around because they're friendly.	4. Here were the spiders—a pleasing kind of bug.	D	FM	A	+ P
5. The only thing which doesn't fit is the grey section at the top because it kind of detracts from the pleasing aspect of it. ∨ Upside down it reminds me of a flower—the 2 sections of it and the, I guess they're called pistils, on the inside—it almost makes me think of a picture of a plant's reproductive system they'd have in a biology book—the grey could be the roots of it all.	5. This green section reminds me of the reproductive system of a flower.	W	FC	Botany	+
6. Actually, it reminds of a uterus and ovaries as well.	6. The same section reminds me of a uterus. (b) Just the general shape.	D	F	At	+

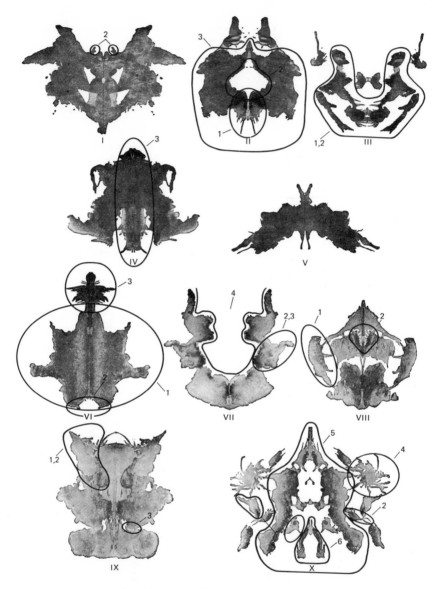

Fig. 12-1. Location sheet for Protocol #1.

Protocol #1
Summary Sheet

		Location	Deter-minants	Content	Form Level	Populars—Originals	Percept
1.	1.	W(S)	F	A	+	P	Butterfly
10″	2.	d	M	Hd	+		Hands
	3.	W(S)	F	(Ad)	+		Mask
	4.	W(S)	Fm	(Ad)	+		Mask
Add.	5.	W(S)	F	(Hd)	+		Pumpkin
II.	1.	D	F	A	+	P	Butterfly
5″	2.	S	F	Spaceship	+		Spaceship
	3.	W	FM·Fc	A	+	P	Bears
Add.	4.	W	F	(Ad)	+		Mask
III.	1.	W	M	H	+	P	Waiters
5″	2.	W	M	H	+		Africans
IV.	1.	W	M·Fc	(A)	+		Monster
13″	2.	W	Fc	Plant	+		Leaves
	3.	D	F	Plant	+		Stem
V.	1.	W	F	A	+	P	Bat
8″							
VI.	1.	W	F	A_{obj}	+	P	Skin
12″	2.	de	M	(Hd)	+		Something reaching
	3.	D	F	(H)	+		Totem pole
VII.	1.	W	M	H	+	P	Women
6″	2.	D	Fc	(H)	+		Gargoyles
	3.	D	F	A	+		Elephants
	4.	S	F	Obj	+		Decanter
VIII.	1.	D	F	A	+	P	Rodents
20″	2.	D(S)	F	At	+	P	Vertebrae
IX.	1.	D	FM·Fm	(A)	+		Unicorn
24″	2.	D	FC	A	+		Lobster
	3.	D	M	Hd	+		Fingers
X.	1.	W	Fm	Nature	+		Garden
5″	2.	D	FC	A	+		Beetles
	3.	D	FC	A	+		Birds
	4.	D	FM	A	+	P	Spiders
	5.	W	FC	Botany	+		Flower
	6.	D	F	At	+		Uterus

Protocol #1
Tabulation Sheet

Location		Determinants			Content	
W	5(+1)	F	13(+2)		H	3
W(S)	3(+1)	M	6		(H)	2
W	5	FM	1		Hd	2(+1)
		Fm	2		(Hd)	1
D	13	Fc	2			
D(S)	1	FC	4		A	10
		Multiple	3		(A)	2
d	1	Deter-			(Ad)	2(+1)
de	1	minants				
		FM·Fc,	M·Fc,	FM·Fm	At	2
S	2				Masks	2
					Plant	2

Number of responses	31(+2)	W:M	13:7
Rejections: Cards		Sum C	2
Number of populars	10	M:sum C	7:2
Number of originals		m:c	6:4
Average R/T chromatic	11.8"	VIII-X%	35
Average R/T achromatic	9.8"	FK+F+Fc%	55
F%	42	(H+A):(Hd+Ad)	17:5
F+%	100		
A%	45		
H%	26		

Apperception   W 42%   D 45%   d 3%   Dd+S 10%

Intellectual level   Superior

PSYCHOLOGICAL TEST REPORT

NAME: Linda   **AGE:**   38   **DATE:**   10/19/79

Test Administered

Rorschach Test.

Behavioral Observations

Linda was neatly dressed, as is appropriate to her job as a guidance counselor in a parochial school. She was friendly and helpful to the examiner, offering coffee both before and after the testing. She displayed a small amount of tension before the testing began but this dissipated during the course of the session. She referred several times to the emotional or aesthetic impact the cards had on her, with statements such as, "This isn't very appealing." She had volunteered to take the Rorschach, and stated afterward that it had been an interesting experience; she thanked the examiner sincerely.

Interpretation of Test Findings

Linda is currently operating at an intellectual level of average to very superior ($A\% = 45$, $W = 13$). However, her limited range of interests and lack of flexibility in her approach to new situations interferes with an optimum realization of her intellectual potential ($A\% = 45$, $F\% = 42$). She tends to rely upon an overemphasis on conventionality ($P = 10$), although she is capable of being receptive and responsive to the outside world ($R = 31$), at least in a mechanical way (sum $C = 2$). She is able to handle practical problems ($D\% = 45$), and shows good organizational ability ($W\% = 42$), but perhaps overemphasizes global approaches at the expense of attending to small details ($d\% = 3$). Although she has an active fantasy life (Card VII – gargoyle, Card IX – unicorn), her intellectual ties to reality are unwavering ($F + \% = 100$). She displays a level of aspiration appropriate to her abilities ($W:M = 13:7$) and is able to draw on her inner resources when necessary (7 M's, M's usually good form). Apparently finding her impulse life threatening, Linda is quick to impose intellectual controls on her affective reactions, which results in a lack of spontaneity (14 A's to 8 H's, but only 5 FM's to 7 M's—therefore avoids use of FM much more than M, sum $C = 2$, all FC). This suppression and denial of both the awareness and expression of impulses contributes to conflict and tension, with impulses striving to be acknowledged perceived as destructive outside forces which threaten the organization of her personality (Fm = 3). She appears to be struggling to maintain her personality integrity in the face of these forces. This inner conflict and related feelings of vulnerability prevent her from fully attaining her creative potential, and lead her to respond to new situations in a stereotyped way, at least initially (F responses usually given first).

This conflict also prevents Linda from fully attending to the outer world, especially in terms of its emotional impact (F = 13, sum C = 2). Her self-control is achieved at the expense of emotional involvement (M:sum C = 7:2, F% = 42). She often views the world in an impersonal light (F% = 42), although her interpersonal sensitivity (Fc = 4) does allow her, at least superficially, friendly relationships (F% = 42, FK + F + Fc% = 55, CF = 0). It is difficult for her to respond to emotional stimuli in general (longest RT to Cards VIII and IX), and she experiences particular inability to deal effectively with emerging dysphoric feelings (partial rejection of Card V). She is intellectually self-assertive and may also tend to be somewhat self-critical (W(S) + D(S) + S = 5, (H) = 2, Hd = 2, (Hd) = 1).

Linda's self-preoccupation gives rise to a degree of impairment in object relations (threatening masks on Cards I and II, monster on Card IV). Consistent with the fact that she is in a religious order which demands chastity is evidence of a lack of interest in, and/or fear of emotional involvement with men (perceived Card IV as "menacing," had trouble seeing anything in Card IV at all, cut off the phallic part of Card VI instead of integrating it into a W response). On the other hand, some concern with the general issue of generativity and childbearing is apparent (reproductive system responses to Card X).

There are several significant indications that Linda is experiencing strong needs to make changes in her life. She is aware of her need for the acceptance and approval of others and has accepted this need (Fc = 4, mostly furry). She is also aware that this need has been frustrated in the past (subjective shading disturbance), and that emotional stimulation can be pleasant (positive comment on colors of Card IX). Within the framework of her good social skills (FC = 4, FC:CF + C = 4:0) and empathetic ability (7M, 3H) she is frequently able to lower her defenses in social situations (less constricted in Inquiry phase than Association phase). Most reflective of her strivings for greater interpersonal and affective gratification is her response to Card I: "two hands reaching out on top." In the same vein on Card VI, she saw: "at the top something . . . part of the object but yet going beyond the limits of the object—going beyond what's there, reaching out." Finally, one of her percepts to Card IX was: "It looks like the green with these fingers on the bottom is reaching out to the pink or wanting to include it in some way." She clearly feels a need to "go beyond the limits" of her comparatively constricted personality and, from the rest of her record, it appears likely that she has the emotional strength and inner resources to do so.

Summary and Recommendations

Linda is an intelligent, well-organized woman with good inner resources. However, at this time she is overcontrolled and there is conflict over the expression of her feelings and impulses. While she has more adequate social skills, she feels easily threatened and vulnerable in interpersonal situations and may, therefore, generally limit the degree of her involvement with others. She is currently experiencing a sense of personal dissatisfaction and is engaged in a process of self-assessment with justified confidence that she can identify assets that will enable her to derive more gratification from her interactions with the environment. This client would have a good prognosis in counseling, should she be so inclined.

Protocol #2
Rorschach Response Form for Ida; 44 Years Old: 2/3/77

I. 10″	1.	What people eat—I only know the word in German—cra**b**. (Some people see more than one thing. Do you see anything else?).	1. It makes me think of food (What does food call to mind?). Food is poisoned. (What do you mean?). I'm always afraid that food is poisoned—even I thought that bananas are injected with poison—I never taste food from a stranger or someone I don't know very well.	W	A	+	
	2.	"Adler" in German—an eagle.	2. High in the air. (What does that call to mind?). An airplane. (What does an airplane make you think of?). Having a crash—I'm always afraid that airplanes will crash.	W	A	+	
II. 22″	1.	I don't see anything—I have no imagination. I'd say it's an animal.	1. An animal can be a sweet thing—and it can be a beast—like lions in a jungle—when kept in a house—it's very sweet and loving. (What does does that bring to mind?). Depression.	D	A	+	
	2.	A dog.	2. They're kissing each other. (What does that bring to mind?). Sex. (What does that make you think of?). Masturbation. Some people masturbate because they can't get fulfillment with other people. (What does that make you think of in your own life?). A doctor once when I was 19 asked if I masturbated and I said I don't know what it is—I went home and tried it out. It was a stupid question—he made me do it.	D	A	+	P

	Response	Inquiry				
III. 25″ 1.	Two persons playing ball.	Childhood. (What does that make you think of?). Loneliness (?). I never had any friends. (Why?). Because I was with foster parents—I had a lot of food I didn't want—I never was hungry, I never wanted to eat (Find one more thing that this blot might look like). They don't have heads like persons—they're like animals in caricature. (What does that make you think of?). They're good-natured.	W	H	+	P+
IV. 45″ 1.	This 11 2 pairs of boots.	A pair of boots is sadistic. (What does that make you think of?). Getting hit. (What does that call to mind?). When I was 7, a mother always was spanking her little girl with a stick—I imagined I was her.	D	Obj	+	P
2.	That—I DK what it is—It 11 a jumpsuit.	It's itchy—every material bothers me. (What does that remind you of?). Wool. I could never wear wool—I was forced screaming into wool sweaters—I couldn't wear them.	W	Obj	+	
V. 35″ 1.	2 pieces of meat.	Makes me think of throwing it in the toilet. When I was a little girl, I threw it in the toilet. I could never eat meat. (What does your not eating meat call to mind?). It could get stuck in my throat, and people die. (Find one more thing that this blot might resemble.) It looks like a butterfly. (What does a butterfly remind you of?) Pulling out their wings when	W	Food		

(continued)

115

VI. 26″ 1.	A butterfly.	I was a little girl. (What does that remind you of?) I was a sadistic fiend I guess—generally I'm very kind to animals.	W	A	+
	1.	No—I didn't pull out their wings—I would catch them, put them in a box, and give them food—I never pulled out their wings. (Find one more thing that this blot might look like.) It's shaped like a leaf. (What does that make you think of?) Plants and growing—plants never grow in my apartment—there's always darkness in my apartment.	W	A	+
VII. 55″ 1.	I'd say animals—but there's a tail up on their head—they don't look right.	1. I don't know—it doesn't make sense.	D	A	+
2.	It could be a dance on the snow.	2. Falling down. (What does that make you think of in your own life?) I was falling down when I was ice-skating—I never went on the ice again.	D	Na	
3.	This all 11 embryos to me. All the cards 11 this.	3. Children. (What does that make you think of?) I'm glad I don't have any—I'm sick, I can't give them an education—I'm glad I don't have children, but I love them very much.	D	(H)	
VIII. 3″ 1.	This is a skeleton of a human body.	1. A dead person. (What does that make you think of?) My father died before I was born—I still love him. (What does that call to mind?) A lot of sadness—for my mother too—she then didn't want to have me any-	W	A+	−

Card	No.	Response	Inquiry	Loc	Det	Score
			more. (Find one more thing that the blot might resemble.) 2 fishes. (What do they make you think of?) Nothing special—a fish has to be in the water. There are some very nice fish around. I don't like to eat fish because they have bones.	d	Obj	—
IX. 50″	1.	This is a candle.	1. Romance. In restaurants when I was younger—I used to be very happy. (What does that remind you of?) Being in love—it's a wonderful feeling.	W	Bot	+
	2.	A glass vase with water, flowers are around.	2. It's just romantic.	D	Bot	
X. 15″	1.	They all have the same shape. This flower.	1. Makes me think of being in love—a person gets flowers when they're in love—a beautiful garden of flowers in the sun. (What does such a garden make you think of in your own life?) There will always be darkness in my life—except for childhood. But I didn't want to go into the garden—I always wanted to be in the room—It was safer.	D		
	2.	An insect.	2. An insect—a bee who has bitten me several times in the garden—I had a swollen foot and I couldn't go to school.	D	A	+

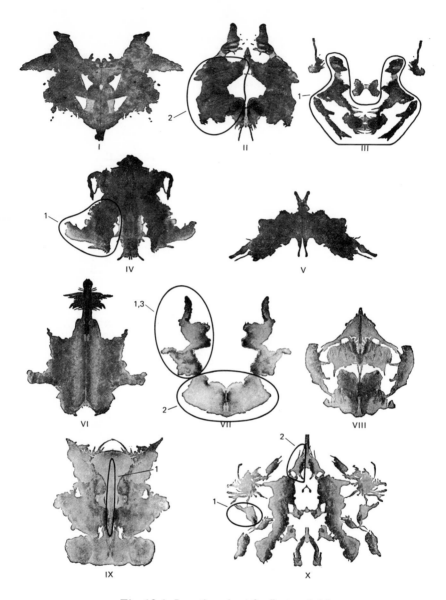

Fig. 12-1. Location sheet for Protocol #2.

Protocol #2
Summary Sheet

		Location	Content	Form Level	Populars—Originals	Percept
I.	1.	W	A	+		Crab
10″	2.	W	A	+		Eagle
II.	1.	W	A	−		Animal
22″	2.	D	A	+	P	dog
III.	1.	W	H	+	P	People playing ball
25″						
IV.	1.	D	Obj	+	P	Pair of boots
45″	2.	W	Obj	+		Jumpsuit
V.	1.	W	Food			Pieces of meat
35″						
VI.	1.	W	A	−		Butterfly
26″						
VII.	1.	D	A	+		Animal
55″	2.	D	Nat			Snow
	3.	D	(H)			Embryo
VIII.	1.	W	At	−		Skeleton
3″						
IX.	1.	d	Obj	+		Candle
50″	2.	W	Bot	−		Vase of flowers
X.	1.	D	Bot			Flower
15″	2.	D	A	+		Insect

Protocol #2
Tabulation Sheet

	Location		Content	
W	9	H	1	
D	7	(H)	1	
d	1	A	7	

Number of responses	17	Average R/T achromatic	34.2
Rejections: Cards	0	A%	41
Number of populars	3	H%	12
Number of originals	0	VIII-X%	29
Average R/T chromatic	21.6		

Apperception   W 53%   D 41%   d 6%

PSYCHOLOGICAL TEST REPORT

Name: ___Ida___   **Age:** __44__   **Date:** __2/3/77__

Tests Administered

Rorschach Test, WAIS, TAT, Bender Gestalt test, Rotter Incomplete Sentences Blank, Psychological Data sheet, Figure Drawing.*

History and Background Information

This patient first came to a hospital in 1965 at which time she was described as suspicious of people, withdrawn, unable to do office work. The patient has had two hospitalizations in the past.

The patient was born in Germany; her father died before her birth. The mother was reportedly depressed, and suffered "bad health" after the patient's birth. A stepsister was reported to have had arguments with the mother about boyfriends. The patient liked this sister, who was attentive to her. In 1940, the patient was evacuated from Germany to a foster home in another country because of the war. The patient states that she later learned that a further reason for this evacuation was the fact that her mother was half-Jewish. The patient states that, "I was very unhappy about being sent away and thought at that time that my mother had abandoned me." A "key scene" she recalls from her childhood involved her foster mother telling her that she did not love the patient anymore.

The patient's schooling was interrupted as a result of the war; she states that she terminated school in the eighth grade. She held various typing and secretarial jobs following the war, arriving in the United States in 1959. Since that time, she worked as a secretary. The patient is single and has never married.

The patient states that she has a "sleeping problem" and usually doesn't get up before 1 o'clock. "Sometimes I stay in bed all day because I feel sick." The patient complains of severe headaches, palpitations, and sweating. She also describes herself as withdrawn, with minimal social life.

Behavioral Observations

The patient is a tall, thin woman who arrived well and appropriately dressed for her test session. She spoke English with a thick German accent; she spoke in a flat, emotionless voice throughout the session.

---

*To demonstrate the applications of the Content Rorschach, only the WAIS and the Rorschach are used to document interpretive statements in this illustrative case report.

The patient immediately began excusing her performance as testing began. She stated that she was "not a good talker," had no imagination, was very sick, had little education, etc., and that the examiner would have to take these facts into account. She often gave up easily on tasks; she would sometimes continue if the examiner insisted.

The patient had little emotional contact with the examiner; she avoided eye contact and largely just responded to questions and directions. She was, however, observant of what went on in the session. At one point, when the examiner took out a handkerchief, she blurted out, "Do you have a cold?" While the patient generally avoided interacting with the examiner, when testing was concluded, she gave a shy smile and shook the examiner's hand before leaving.

The patient completed all tasks presented to her. She also took several tests home with her and later returned them; she typed in extensive answers to questions about her background history.

Interpretation of Test Findings

On the WAIS, the patient obtained a verbal IQ of 78, a performance IQ of 70, and a full-scale IQ of 73. This places her present level of intellectual functioning in the borderline mental defective range.

From her scores on sub-tests, however, it seems likely that her pre-morbid level of functioning lies in the average range. Her scores were considerably lowered by the high degree of confusion present at this time, by her different cultural background, by her relatively low level of education, and also by her poor frustration tolerance. The patient performed best on tasks involving some social skills. Her ability to abstract and her capacity to distinguish essential from unessential details are also among the best preserved of her abilities.

Ego functioning is problematic at times. Reality testing sometimes fails under stress (extended F+%), resulting in distorted perceptions of the environment. Object relations also show some impairment (low H%, past and present described social isolation—e.g., see comment regarding few childhood friends on Card III). There is also evidence of difficulty maintaining the defense of repression, resulting in the eruption of inappropriate and sometimes primitive material into consciousness (masturbation comments on response II - 1, comment on Card VII that "all the cards look like embryos," presence of Rorschach confabulations).

The patient is an individual who has been deeply scarred by the early events of her life (repeated references to trauma in associations to percepts). While she longs for close relationships with people, she also associates "oral supplies" with danger and hurt ("poison" association to food on Card I, negative association to food on Card III, reference to food getting stuck in the throat on Card V). It seems likely that the patient's perceived rejection by her mother and her stepparents is connected with her reluctance to accept affection (reference to rejection by both parents on Card VIII - 1). The patient consequently insulates herself from potential hurt with her guarded, insulated defensive style ("crab" as her first Rorschach percept, almost phobic reaction to wool sweaters on Card IV - 2, and patient's general demeanor during testing).

While the patient is frightened of receiving affection and attention from others, she is also unfortunately in the position of wanting it desperately. She appears to still manage to get gratifications from others in two ways. Firstly, the patient seems to find it acceptable to get sympathy and concern from people through her "sickness," i.e., through display of symptoms, both mental and physical. Secondly, the patient seems to be gratified by attention from others that is accomplished by aggression; a sadomasochistic orientation is seen (comments on IV - 1, V - 1, and VI - 1 about sadistic boots and tearing the wings off butterflies). An early association of physical abuse with parental attentiveness is reported (comments on IV - 1 about envying a girl who was being spanked).

The patient has difficulty accepting her basic drives, both sexual and aggressive in nature (airplane crashing on Card I - 2, and nonacceptance of masturbation on Card II - 2). A primary means by which she deals with her unacceptable impulses is through the defense of projection, resulting in the paranoid flavor that suffuses her test record (eagle and poisoned food comment on Card I, projection seen in masturbation associations in response II - 2).

Significant depression is seen. The patient clearly experiences her present life as rather cold and unsatisfying (comments about plants not growing for her, snowdance, and darkness in her life in responses VI - 1, VII - 2, and X - 1, respectively). However, it should also be noted that some hope and potential for better social and general life functioning are present (more optimistic associations and comments on cards IX and X, patient's tentative "engaging" with the examiner at the conclusion of testing).

While the patient "uses" her sickness to get attention and caring from others, and may thus tend to magnify her complaints, those working with her must recognize that she is nonetheless fragile and seriously disturbed. At times, the distinction between reality and fantasy is blurred for this patient (contradictory comments about whether she tore the wings off butterflies on Cards V and VI). The general diagnostic impression is one of schizophrenia, paranoid-type.

Summary and Recommendations

This patient's verbal IQ of 78, performance IQ of 70, and full-scale IQ of 73 place her present level of intellectual functioning in the borderline mental defective range. Mental confusion, poor frustration tolerance, a low level of schooling, and her cultural background are all contributants to these low scores. Her premorbid level appears to lie in the average range. Ego functioning is poor, with problems seen in reality testing, object relations, and the maintenance of repression. Perceptual disturbances associated with schizophrenia are present.

This patient is deeply distrustful of others. She has withdrawn from relationships to narcissistic self-preoccupation. She rejects oral supplies from others, which is probably traceable to early rejection by her mother. While she is frightened of the oral supplies, she still craves them. She accepts attention from others through sympathy for her symptoms and when the attention she wants is linked with aggression (i.e., through masochism on her part). She has great difficulty accepting her basic sexual and aggressive drives, projecting them onto others, resulting in strong paranoid trends. While her desire for sympathy from others may result in her magnifying her symptoms, it must be kept in mind that she is nonetheless fragile and seriously disturbed. The diagnostic impression is one of schizophrenia, paranoid type.

The patient needs a long-term psychotherapy relationship with a supportive therapist who can gradually bring her out of her shell while at the same time shoring up ego defenses. Her therapist should continually be aware of the fragility of this patient's adjustment. Participation in a supportive socialization group might also be considered at some point, given her loneliness and her desire for closer relationships with other people. Biofeedback might also be considered as an adjunctive procedure for her headaches; however, the use to which she puts her physical symptoms must also be kept in mind.

References

Alcock, T. *The Rorschach in practice*. Philadelphia: J. P. Lippincott, 1963.

Allen, R. M. *Student's Rorschach manual*. New York: International Universities Press, 1954.

Allport, G. W. *Personality: A psychological interpretation*. New York: Henry Holt & Company, 1937.

Allport, G. W. *Pattern and growth in personality*. New York: Holt, Rinehart & Winston, 1961.

Ames, L. B. Are Rorschach responses influenced by society's change? *Journal of Personality Assessment*, 1975, *39*, 439–452.

Ames, L. B., Metraux, R. W., Rodell, J. L., & Walker, R. N. *Rorschach responses in old age* (rev. ed.). New York: Brunner-Mazel, 1973.

Ames, L. B., Metraux, R. W., Rodell, J. L., & Walker, R. N. *Child Rorschach responses* (rev. ed.). New York: Brunner-Mazel, 1974.

Ames, L. B., Metraux, R. W., & Walker, R. N. *Adolescent Rorschach responses* (rev. ed.). New York: Brunner-Mazel, 1971.

Anastasi, A. *Psychological testing* (4th ed.). New York: Macmillan, 1976.

Appelbaum, S. A. The effect of altered psychological atmosphere on Rorschach responses: A new supplementary procedure. In M. Kornrich (Ed.), *Psychological test modifications*. Springfield, Ill.: Charles C. Thomas, 1965. (Reprinted from *Bulletin of the Menninger Clinic*, 1959, *23*, 179–189.)

Aronow, E., & Reznikoff, M. *Rorschach content interpretation*. New York: Grune & Stratton, 1976.

Arthur, B. The forced confabulation technique: An extension of the Rorschach method for use with children. In M. Kornrich (Ed.), *Psychological test modifications*. Springfield, Ill.: Charles C. Thomas, 1965.

Beck, S. J., Beck, A. C., Levitt, E. E., & Molish, H. B. *Rorschach's test I. Basic processes* (3rd ed.). New York: Grune & Stratton, 1961.

De Vos, G. A quantitative approach to affective symbolism in Rorschach responses. *Journal of Projective Techniques*, 1952, *16*, 133–150.

Elizur, A. Content analysis of the Rorschach with regard to anxiety and hostility. *Rorschach Research Exchange and Journal of Projective Techniques*, 1949, *13*, 247–284.

Elitzur, B. Content analysis of the Rorschach in two phases: Imaginary story and self interpretation. *Perceptual and Motor Skills*, 1976, *43*, 43–46.

Ellenberger, H. The life and work of Hermann Rorschach (1884–1922). *Bulletin of the Menninger Clinic*, 1954, *18*, 173–219.

Endicott, N. A. The Holtzman inkblot technique content measures of depression and suspiciousness. *Journal of Personality Assessment*, 1972, *36*, 424–426.

Eron, L. D. Review of the Rorschach. In O. K. Buros (Ed.), *The sixth mental measurements yearbook*. Highland Park, N.J.: Gryphon Press, 1965.

Exner, J. E. *The Rorschach: A comprehensive system*. New York: John Wiley & Sons, 1974.

Fisher, S., & Cleveland, S. E. *Body image and personality* (2nd ed.). New York: Dover, 1968.

Francis-Williams, J. *Rorschach with children*. London: Pergamon Press, 1968.

Halpern, F. *A clinical approach to children's Rorschachs*, New York: Grune & Stratton, 1953.

Halpern, F. The Rorschach test with children. In A. I. Rabin & M. R. Haworth (Eds.), *Projective techniques with children*. New York: Grune & Stratton, 1960.

Halpern, H. M. A Rorschach interview technique: Clinical validation of the examiner's hypotheses. In M. Kornrich (Ed.), *Psychological test modifications*. Springfield, Ill.: Charles C. Thomas, 1965. (Reprinted from *Journal of Projective Techniques*, 1957, *21*, 10–17.)

Hammer, M. A comparison of responses by clinic and normal adults to Rorschach card III human figure area. *Journal of Projective Techniques and Personality Assessment*, 1966, *30*, 161–162.

Hershenson, J. R. Preferences of adolescents for Rorschach figures. *Child Development*, 1949, *20*, 101–118.

Hertz, M. R. *Frequency tables for scoring Rorschach responses* (5th ed.). Cleveland: Press of Case Western Reserve University, 1970.

Hertz, M. R. The method of administration of the Rorschach ink-blot test. *Child Development*, 1936, *7*, 237–254.

Hertzman, M., & Pearce, J. The personal meaning of the human figure in the Rorschach. *Psychiatry*, 1947, *10*, 413–422.

Holt, R. R., & Havel, J. A method for assessing primary and secondary process in the Rorschach. In M. A. Rickers-Ovsiankina (Ed.), *Rorschach psychology*. New York: John Wiley & Sons, 1960.

Huber, J. T. *Report writing in psychology and psychiatry*. New York: Harper, 1961.

Janis, M. G., & Janis, I. L. A supplementary test based on free association to Rorschach responses. In M. Kornrich (Ed.), *Psychological test modifications*. Springfield, Ill.: Charles C. Thomas, 1965. (Reprinted from *Rorschach Research Exchange*, 1946, *10*, 1–19.)

Kessel, P., Harris, J. E., & Slagle, S. J. An associative technique for analyzing the content of Rorschach test responses. *Perceptual and Motor Skills*, 1969, *29*, 535–540.

Klopfer, B., Ainsworth, M. D., Klopfer, W. G., & Holt, R. R. *Developments in the Rorschach technique, Vol. I: technique and theory.* New York: Harcourt, Brace & World, 1954.

Klopfer, B., & Davidson, H. H. *The Rorschach technique: An introductory manual.* New York: Harcourt, Brace & World, 1962.

Klopfer, B., Fox, J., & Troup, E. Problems in the use of the Rorschach technique with children. In B. Klopfer (Ed.), *Developments in the Rorschach technique, Vol. II.* New York: Harcourt, Brace & World, 1956.

Klopfer, W. G. *The psychological report.* New York: Grune & Stratton, 1960.

Kornrich, M. Eliciting "new" Rorschach responses. In M. Kornrich (Ed.), *Psychological test modifications.* Springfield, Ill.: Charles C. Thomas, 1965.

Leventhal, T., Slepian, H. J., Gluck, M. R., & Rosenblatt, B. P. The utilization of the psychologist-patient relationship in diagnostic testing. *Journal of Projective Techniques,* 1962, *26,* 66–79.

Levitt, E. E., & Truumaa, A. *The Rorschach technique with children and adolescents.* New York: Grune & Stratton, 1972.

Mindess, H. The symbolic dimension. In B. Klopfer, M. M. Meyer, F. B. Brawer, & W. G. Klopfer (Eds.), *Developments in the Rorschach technique* (Vol. 3). New York: Harcourt Brace Jovanovich, 1970.

Molish, H. B. The popular response in Rorschach records of normals, neurotics, and schizophrenics. *American Journal of Orthopsychiatry,* 1951, *21,* 523–531.

Pascal, G. R., Ruesch, H. A., Devine, C. A., & Suttell, B. J. A study of genital symbols on the Rorschach test: Presentation of a method and results. *Journal of Abnormal and Social Psychology,* 1950, *45,* 286–295.

Phillips, L., & Smith, J. G. *Rorschach interpretation: Advanced technique.* New York: Grune & Stratton, 1953.

Potkay, C. R. *The Rorschach clinician.* New York: Grune & Stratton, 1971.

Powers, W. T., & Hamlin, R. M. The validity, bases, and process of clinical judgment, using a limited amount of projective test data. *Journal of Projective Techniques,* 1957, *21,* 286–293.

Reznikoff, M., Aronow, E., & Rauchway, A. The reliability of inkblot content scales. In C. D. Spielberger & J. D. Butcher (Eds.), *Advances in personality assessment* (Vol. 1). Hillsdale, N.J.: Erlbaum, 1982.

Schachtel, E. G. *Experiential foundations of Rorschach's test.* New York: Basic Books, 1966.

Schafer, R. *Psychoanalytic interpretation in Rorschach testing.* New York: Grune & Stratton, 1954.

Schafer, R. *The clinical application of psychological tests.* New York: International Universities Press, 1948.

Stevens, S. S. *Handbook of experimental psychology.* New York: John Wiley & Sons, 1951.

Symonds, P. M. A contribution to our knowledge of the validity of the Rorschach. *Journal of Projective Techniques,* 1955, *19,* 152–162.

Tallent, N. *Psychological report writing.* Englewood Cliffs, N.J.: Prentice-Hall, 1975.

Wheeler, W. M. An analysis of Rorschach indices of male homosexuality. *Rorschach Research Exchange and Journal of Projective Techniques*, 1949, *13*, 97–126.

Zimmerman, I. L., Lambert, N. M., & Class, L. A comparison of children's perceptions of Rorschach cards III, IV, and VII with independent ratings of parental adequacy, and effectiveness of school behavior. *Psychology in the Schools*, 1966, *3*, 258–263.

Zubin, J. The non-projective aspects of the Rorschach experiment: I. Introduction. *Journal of Social Psychology*, 1956, *44*, 179–192.

Zubin, J., Eron, L. D., & Schumer, F. *An Experimental approach to projective techniques*. New York: John Wiley & Sons, 1965.

REFERENCE NOTE

1. Burt, C. *The Rorschach test*. Unpublished manuscript, University College, London, 1945.

Index

Page numbers in *italics* indicate illustrations.